MAX WEBER'S METHODOLOGY

MAX WEBER'S METHODOLOGY

THE UNIFICATION OF THE
CULTURAL AND SOCIAL SCIENCES

—

FRITZ RINGER

Harvard University Press
Cambridge, Massachusetts
London, England

First Harvard University Press paperback edition, 2000

Library of Congress Cataloging-in-Publication Data

Ringer, Fritz K., 1934–
Max Weber's methodology : the unification of the cultural and
social sciences / Fritz Ringer.
p. cm.
Includes bibliographical references and index.
ISBN 0-674-55657-7 (cloth)
ISBN 0-674-00183-4 (pbk.)
1. Weber, Max, 1864–1920—Contributions in social sciences.
I. Title.
H59.W4R56   1997
300—dc21   97-21685

For Monica

CONTENTS

—

Acknowledgments   *ix*

Introduction: Interpretation and Explanation   *1*

1 Aspects of Weber's Intellectual Field   7
    The German Historical Tradition   *8*
    The Threat of 'Positivism'   *17*
    The Revival of the Humanistic Disciplines   *26*

2 Weber's Adaptation of Rickert   36
    Rickert's Position and Its Problems   *36*
    Weber's Adaptation   *45*
    Against Naturalism, Holism, and Irrationalism   *52*

3 Singular Causal Analysis   63
    Objective Probability and Adequate Causation   *63*
    The Frameworks and Tactics of Causal Analysis   *72*
    Contemporary Formulations   *80*

4 Interpretation and Explanation   92
    From Interpretation to Causal Analysis   *92*
    Interpretive Sociology   *100*
    The Ideal Type and Its Functions   *110*

5 Objectivity and Value Neutrality   122
    The Two Components of Weber's Position through 1910   *122*
    The Maxim and Ethos of Value Neutrality   *131*
    Contemporary Formulations   *142*

6 From Theory to Practice 150

Neither Marxism nor Idealism 150

*From Methodological Individualism to the Comparative
    Analysis of Structural Change* 155

An Example of Weber's Practice: The Protestant Ethic 163

Conclusion 168

Bibliography 177

Index 185

ACKNOWLEDGMENTS

—

Much of the work on this book was done while I was a member of the dashing class of 1993–94 at the National Humanities Center, a beautiful place with a marvelous staff. The writing was properly launched under a Guggenheim Fellowship in the fall of 1994.

I would particularly like to thank those who helped me with discerning readings of the manuscript. My colleague Wesley Salmon read Chapter 3. Donald Fleming of Harvard University read the entire draft, as did my former students Paul Vogt of the State University of New York at Albany, John McCole of the University of Oregon, and two current doctoral students at the University of Pittsburgh and Carnegie Mellon University—Leslie Hammond and Julia Roos—who concentrated on the Notes and the Bibliography. Finally, I am grateful to Terry Soffa, who manages my paperwork along with much of my professional life.

MAX WEBER'S METHODOLOGY

INTRODUCTION: INTERPRETATION
AND EXPLANATION

—

One of Max Weber's greatest achievements was his integration of two divergent perspectives that have divided theorists and practitioners of the historical, social, and cultural sciences since the nineteenth century.[1] The barrier between these two approaches was particularly high in Weber's own academic culture, but it has also appeared in other ages and scholarly contexts. Indeed, its remnants remain serious obstacles to thought in our own intellectual environment. To identify Weber's methodological project as the unification of the cultural and social sciences is thus to take a position on certain current issues as well.

The two lines of analysis may be called the 'interpretive' and the 'explanatory' approaches, and of the two, the interpretive one was certainly dominant in Weber's own world. According to that tradition, the chief task of the historian or student of culture is the 'hermeneutic' or interpretive understanding *(Verstehen)* of human 'meanings.' Thus historical actions are to be understood—not causally explained—in relation to the agents' intentions and beliefs. Texts, cultures, and historical epochs are to be conceived as systems of interrelated meanings or concepts, systems that can be elucidated only 'internally,' 'in their own terms.' Like other scholarly tradi-

---

1. See the Bibliography for Weber's relevant writings and abbreviations used. Note also that short forms of citation will be used throughout for works more fully described in the Bibliography.

tions, the interpretive line of analysis has been pursued with varying degrees of rigor. Some of its champions have portrayed the under-standing of meanings as an intuitive leap or an empathetic identification. But this subjectivist emphasis has been supplemented or replaced by more complex models of interpretation, with results that can be validated in principle. Like other scholarly traditions, moreover, the interpretive approach has produced impressive exem-plars of scholarly *practice,* even when it has been weakly or mislead-ingly defended in theory.

The explanatory tradition, too, has been richer in its practices than in its methodological codifications. With or without the benefit of theory, for example, historians have long been concerned with the causes of events. Some have distinguished long-term or 'underlying' from short-term or 'precipitating' causes; others have explained par-ticular 'trends' or outcomes in terms of various 'contributing factors.' Such commonsense analytical tactics have prevailed across the whole spectrum of the cultural and social sciences; yet attempts to explicate them have run into problems, including the central difficulty of reconciling theories of explanation with theories of interpretation.

On the whole, spokesmen for the explanatory direction have minimized the methodological differences between the natural and the historical or cultural sciences. Some of them have believed—or been suspected of believing—that the facts about the past could be assembled to yield significant empirical generalizations, or to reveal transcultural regularities, 'constant conjunctions' in the sense of David Hume. A few theorists within the school have sought to ground the explanation of human actions in the 'laws' of psychology or physiology; or they have anticipated that such 'naturalist' strate-gies will succeed in the future. But the clearest 'neo-positivist' program in the contemporary cultural and social sciences is Carl G. Hempel's 'covering law model' of historical explanation. According to the strictest, 'deductive nomological' version of this model, to explain an event is to deduce the statement that it occurred from (a) specified initial conditions and (b) one or more universal laws that 'cover' the case.[2] Hempel has explicitly conceded that explanations

2. Hempel, "Function of General Laws," and "Reasons and Covering Laws."

in human affairs are likely to be imperfect in various ways, usually falling short of the standards required for prediction. Nevertheless, Hempel and other neo-positivists see no *logical* difference between explanations in the natural and the cultural sciences. Some of them have distrusted the interpretationist emphasis upon relations of meaning. In any case, a clear tension between prominent codifications of the explanatory and the interpretive traditions subsists in our own day, and that tension was markedly greater in Weber's own culture.

If Weber nevertheless resolved the tension—and thus achieved the unification of the cultural and social sciences, he did so by means of two crucial reformulations. To begin with, he adopted an intricate and flexible scheme of *singular causal analysis,* a type of analysis in which *particular* events, historical changes, or outcomes are traced to their causally relevant antecedents. The word singular should not be taken to imply a monocausal approach, or an exclusive emphasis upon single individuals or 'basic facts.' Only what is *explained* is singular, and this only in the logical sense that it is not general (like the ideal gas law, or Gresham's law), that it can be more or less specifically identified and located in space and time (like a volcanic eruption, the Defenestration of Prague,[3] or the rise of Western capitalism). Weber's account of singular causal analysis was based upon probabilistic and counterfactual reasoning, not upon deductions from causal laws. His concepts of 'objective probability' and 'adequate causation' cannot be satisfactorily characterized in a few sentences; we will have to come back to them. But his overall conception is one of alternate processes and possible outcomes that are more or less probable, more or less strongly favored by relevant causes. The typical causal question is not whether a particular event necessarily followed upon one or more antecedent conditions, but why a certain historical path or outcome was what it was, *and not something else.* A cause is not a sufficient condition for the occur-

---

3. The Defenestration of Prague took place on May 23, 1618. At a meeting of Protestant rebels, two Catholic governors "were thrown from a window in the palace of Prague," a historical encyclopedia informs us. "They fell seventy feet into a ditch, but escaped with their lives." The incident had something to do with the origins of the Thirty Years War; but I don't know who gave it its wonderful name.

rence of the effect; it is a factor that, in conjunction with other background conditions, is comparatively likely and thus 'adequate' to bring about the outcome, rather than other possible alternatives. The world of the cultural and social sciences is an infinitely complex network of causal relations among particulars. We explain aspects of that world by means of probabilistic and counterfactual comparisons between what has actually happened and what would have happened in the absence of adequate causes—or conjunctions of causes.[4]

Along with this line of analysis, Weber developed a model of interpretation based upon the hypothetical attribution of rationality that dispensed with subjectivist *and* naturalist assumptions, while redefining the interpretive process as a form of singular causal analysis. In the interpretation of past actions, according to Weber, we begin by supposing that the relevant agents rationally pursued appropriate ends. The rationality we thus tentatively attribute to historical actors is typically a form of instrumental, 'technical,' or means-ends rationality, although we also project consistency in the agents' motives and beliefs—along with coherence in the texts of the past. What we thus heuristically ascribe to actors in the past is of course *our* rationality. (It is hard to see what else it could be, at least to begin with.) As we proceed to 'compare' the behaviors we anticipate with the courses of action pursued in reality, we adjust or supplement our models of rational action to take account of (a) divergences between our assumptions or modes of reasoning and those of the agents we seek to understand, and (b) irrational motivations and other intervening factors. Our ultimate objective is to construct a set of possibly heterogeneous motives and beliefs that are jointly adequate to account for the behaviors actually observed. Altogether, the interpretive procedures suggested by Weber closely resemble the probabilistic and counterfactual reasoning he associated with singular causal explanation. In that sense, Weber's model of interpretation *depended upon* his account of singular causal analysis, and *both were needed* to spell out an integrated methodology of the cultural and social sciences.[5]

4. Ringer, "Causal Analysis."
5. Ringer, *Fields of Knowledge,* pp. 18–21.

The close connection between interpretation and explanation in Weber's thought is further illustrated by his recommendation of 'ideal types' as heuristic devices. His ideal types are simplifications or 'one-sidedly' exaggerated characterizations of complex phenomena that can be hypothetically posited and then 'compared' with the realities they are meant to elucidate. Often, the ideal types Weber actually suggested were models of rational action; sometimes, they were patterns or processes traceable to simplified sets of causes. They permitted selected elements within causal or behavioral sequences to be ascribed to specified causes, motives, or beliefs. In any case, one cannot understand Weber's doctrine of ideal types apart from his broader vision of causal analysis and interpretation. For Weber and for us, in sum, ideal types make sense only to the extent that they permit the discriminations and counterfactual 'comparisons' involved in the construction of adequate interpretations or explanations.

In contrast to some recent commentators, I see Weber as a clarifier and occasional critic of the German historical tradition, not as a passive heir. I have elsewhere drawn upon Pierre Bourdieu's writings to define the 'intellectual field' as a constellation of positions that are meaningful only in relation to one another, a constellation further characterized by differences of power or authority, by the opposition between orthodoxy and heterodoxy, and by the role of the cultural preconscious, of tacit 'doxa' that are transmitted by inherited practices, institutions, and social relations. Specifying the vague notion of 'context' in this way, one can see that individuals may stand in a variety of specific relationships to their intellectual and social environment.[6]

Thus all participants in an intellectual field should be expected to share at least some of the implicit assumptions upon which it rests, or some element of the pretheoretical 'habitus' it tends to perpetuate. Yet especially during periods of instability in the intellectual field or in the wider culture, mute doxa may be partly replaced by explicit contests between more or less orthodox and heterodox positions. At such junctures, the most rigorous and unconventional thinkers

6. Ibid., pp. 1–12.

will initiate a process of critical clarification. They will seek to codify and explicate inherited practices, to convert previously mute knowledge into explicit concepts—and thus also occasionally to expose as problematic what was formerly taken for granted. Weber's project, in sum, is best understood as a critical clarification of the German historical and interpretive tradition. He was not just a perpetuator of that tradition, or its champion in the face of 'positivism'; nor can he himself be identified as a 'positivist' in any coherent sense of that term. Rather, as I hope to show, he was at once a causalist and a sophisticated interpretationist, and he simultaneously renewed and transformed his methodological heritage.

Even while trying to 'locate' Weber in his intellectual field along these lines, I will attempt a rational reconstruction of his views in the light of certain *contemporary* texts on the methodology of the human sciences: I will refer to significant present-day accounts of causation and of rational interpretation. Weber himself explicitly recommended the 'ideal typical' use of contemporary models of rational thought as means of reconstructing the texts and belief systems of the past. He saw no conflict—as I see none—between such 'presentist' tactics and the ultimately 'past-minded' or 'contextualist' aim of rigorous interpretation. Indeed, I hope that my readers will find this essay an aid to their own reflections on the questions of method it raises.

Finally, a few words are in order about the relationship between Weber's methodological theories and his substantive work as a comparative historian and social scientist. I must concede that in principle, his theories cannot be fully appreciated apart from his analytical practice. Even his critical relationship to his intellectual field was shaped as much by substantive social and cultural considerations as by methodological issues, and yet this essay will be deliberately restricted to his methodology. I hope eventually to move beyond these artificial limitations in further work on Weber. In the meantime, I want merely to suggest that Weber's substantive achievements were thoroughly grounded in his methodological program.

ASPECTS OF WEBER'S INTELLECTUAL FIELD

1

Sometime around 1800, an educational revolution took place in the German states; it occurred much earlier there than it did in England or France, and it did so long before the industrial revolution reached Germany. One element in this transformation was the emergence of the research imperative, the expectation that university faculty will do original research and prepare their students to do the same. The other crucial component in the revolution was the establishment of educational and professional qualifications for future secondary teachers, and the ultimate introduction of similar credentials for other learned professions as well. In all modern European societies, advanced education eventually became almost as important a source of middle-class self-images as wealth and economic power; but this was true particularly in Germany, where the educational revolution took place earliest and the industrial revolution followed relatively late.

The radical renovation of the universities in Prussia and in other German states during the decades around 1800 assigned an especially important place to the faculties of arts and sciences, or of 'philosophy.' The reform movement was inspired by the new German Idealist philosophy, but also by a neohumanist enthusiasm for classical Greece and by the ideal of *Bildung*, meaning education in the sense of cultivation or personal self-development. While the concept of *Bildung* was of course subject to change over time, it came to represent a fairly stable view of education, and to inform the ideology of the

German *Bildungsbürgertum,* the educated middle class. Thus *Bildung* always referred to the development of the individual's personal potential through an interpretive relationship with great texts. Roughly comparable concepts emerged in other cultures, but in Germany, the ethos of *Bildung* took on an almost metaphysical pathos. Much of German academic culture, Max Weber's intellectual field, can be understood only in the light of the model of *Bildung.* Thus the philological and historical disciplines, not the natural sciences, initially defined the norms of rigorous scholarship in nineteenth-century Germany. The word *Wissenschaft* referred to all forms of systematic knowledge; but a traditional animus against merely 'utilitarian' studies tended to identify 'pure' *Wissenschaft* with theoretical insight and with *Bildung,* rather than with practical intervention in the world. In the language of post-Kantian Idealism, the world exists so that, in coming to know it, the human mind may realize its potential. And in what came to be the German idea of the 'cultural state' *(Kulturstaat),* government found its legitimacy in the intellectual and cultural life it sustained and represented. This too was consistent with the norms of *Bildung.*[1]

The German Historical Tradition

We can begin to understand the German historical tradition that Weber continued and clarified by considering the concept of *Bildung* as it was used in his time. A persistent model of *Bildung* implied that the self-cultivating reader could reproduce or relive *(Erleben)* the experiences or 'values' embodied in his texts, or that he could intuitively identify with their authors.[2] This subjectivist vision helped to sustain the claim that learners were totally transformed by the venerated sources in which they immersed them-

1. Ringer, *Decline of the German Mandarins;* for German originals of texts cited there, see the translation as *Die Gelehrten.* For a summary analysis of *Bildung* as of 1890–1920, see Ringer, *Fields of Knowledge;* for the history of the concept, see esp. Vierhaus, "Bildung."

2. This is explicit, for example, in a dictionary definition from the interwar period. See *Der grosse Brockhaus,* 15th ed. (1928–35) cited in Ringer, *Fields of Knowledge,* pp. 95–96.

selves. Other, methodologically sounder models of interpretation were eventually evolved, including by Weber himself. Yet what may be called *the principle of empathy* long remained a temptation within the German historical tradition. It dictated, for example, that historians must 'put themselves in the place of' the historical agents they seek to understand. Indeed, there is nothing wrong with this injunction, as long as it is understood in a loose and metaphorical sense. Taken literally, however, it implies a process of empathetic reproduction that cannot be communicated or validated. The successful historian becomes a genius, and her powers a mysterious gift. The more she succeeds in identifying with agents in cultures other than her own, moreover, the more she raises what came to be called the 'problem of historism' *(Historismus):* knowing only historically specific world views, we have no reason to exempt our own values and beliefs from the contingent flow of historicity.

The other element in the concept of *Bildung* that helped to shape the German historical tradition may be called the *principle of individuality.* The self-cultivating individual was consistently portrayed as absolutely unique, imbued with a distinctive potential for personal fulfillment.[3] German theories of advanced education thus diverged sharply from a recurrent French emphasis upon the 'socialization' of the younger generation in the light of inherited norms. Nor was *Bildung* conceived as the enhancement of a universal capacity for rationality; it was the development of an incomparable individual. This radical cultural individualism could acquire a utopian significance. It also encouraged a positive view of both individual and cultural diversity; this is the implication that attracted John Stuart Mill to the thought of Wilhelm von Humboldt. Yet the principle of individuality could also make a mystery of the relationship between the incomparable individual and his group or culture.

Thus the religious historian Ernst Troeltsch, one of Weber's most thoughtful contemporaries, placed the "concept of individuality" at the heart of the German Romantic critique of the "mathematical-mechanical West European scientific spirit":

3. Along with notes 1 and 2 above, see Simmel, "Der Begriff und die Tragödie der Kultur," in his *Philosophische Kultur,* p. 248.

The basic constituents of reality are not similar material or social atoms and universal laws . . . but differing unique personalities and individualizing formative forces. . . . The state and society are not created from the individual by way of contract and utilitarian rationality, but from supra-personal spiritual forces that emanate from the most important and creative individuals, the spirit of the people or the religious idea.[4]

Clearly, the principle of individuality excluded additive views of aggregates, including political groupings. Moreover, the commitment to individuality in the study of history made a problem of change. Since 'mechanical' causal processes were excluded, change could only be a teleological unfolding of preexistent potentialities or an "emanation" of intellectual or spiritual forces.

Given the purpose of this essay, I cannot attempt a full account of the German historical tradition.[5] But I can call attention to the thought of a few significant individuals—or to aspects of their thought. Leopold von Ranke was commonly regarded as the dean of nineteenth-century German historians. He attained that status because he rigorously applied the source-critical methods transmitted by the philologists to an unprecedented range of historical sources. He was a great practitioner of the historian's craft. What he mainly recommended in his theoretical and methodological writings was a past-mindedness that recalled the principle of empathy. He wrote of "placing oneself back into [a given] time, into the mind of a contemporary."[6] In line with the concept of the 'cultural state,' moreover, he saw states as the outward embodiments of "intellectual forces," "moral energies" that could be understood only by means of "empathy."[7] That is why his history of interstate relations took its significance from the cultural conflicts they seemed to embody.

4. Troeltsch, *Naturrecht und Humanität*, pp. 13–14, cited in Ringer, *Decline of the German Mandarins*, pp. 100–101.

5. But see Ringer, *Decline of the German Mandarins*, pp. 97–102, and esp. Iggers, *German Conception of History*.

6. Ranke, *Die grossen Mächte*, p. 22.

7. Ibid., p. 60.

At the same time, Ranke persistently championed the principle of individuality. He not only believed that great statesmen and thinkers truly *stood for*, and thus legitimately guided, their nations; he also saw states themselves as "individualities," with their own distinctive "tendencies."[8] Indeed, he repeatedly insisted upon the discontinuity between "the general" and "the particular." "From the particular," he wrote, "you may ascend to the general; but from general theory there is no way back to the intuitive understanding of the particular."[9] What the historian must start from, therefore, is "the unique intellectual and spiritual character of the individual state, its principle."[10] As a profoundly religious thinker, Ranke was able to accept each culture and epoch as utterly distinctive, and yet find meaning in world history as a whole.

Among nineteenth-century German theorists of history, only Johann Gustav Droysen equaled Ranke in authority. Having been available to students in manuscript for some time, his reflections on history were finally printed in 1882.[11] They rested upon a sharp contrast between explanation and interpretive understanding *(Verstehen)*. Droysen associated the latter with intuitive insight, but also with the recovery of past human actions and beliefs from the "traces" they have left in the present. Like Wilhelm Dilthey after him, Droysen distinguished between processes "internal" to the human agent from their outward "expressions."[12] The point of historical inquiry, he argued, is our need to orient ourselves in the "moral world," finding a meaningful link between our past and our future. Much like Hegel, Droysen insisted that "the state is not the sum of the individuals it encompasses; nor does it arise from their wills or exist for the sake of their wills." Adapting the neohumanist and Idealist theory of *Bildung,* he described the course of history as "humanity's coming to consciousness."[13]

8. Ranke, *Das politische Gespräch,* p. 25.
9. Ibid., p. 22.
10. Ibid., p. 19.
11. Droysen, *Grundriss der Historik,* pp. 415–488.
12. Ibid., pp. 422–424.
13. Ibid., pp. 435, 441–444.

Droysen developed some of his views in opposition to H. T. Buckle's two-volume *History of Civilization in England* (1858–1861), which sought to transform history in the image of the natural sciences.[14] Droysen sharply criticized this project, partly on the grounds that it left no room for human agency and free will. But his main argument had to do with the divide between the scientist's search for regularities and the historian's predominant concern with the interpretive understanding of the unique and particular: "The natural sciences . . . see only the same and the unchanging in the transformations they observe. . . . In the individual being, they see . . . no more than either a class concept or a mediator of chemical change. . . . They have neither room nor a term for the concept of purpose."[15] These formulations begin to suggest how the issues of 'positivism' and determinism appeared to German historians during the late nineteenth century.

Max Weber did not comment upon the writings of Ranke or Droysen. But he did review a book closer to his own early research specialization in economic history. This was a famous 1853 opus by Karl Knies, a cofounder of what came to be called the 'older' German historical school of economics. Following in the footsteps of Friedrich von Savigny and the German historical school of law, Knies and a handful of precursors, including Wilhelm Roscher, launched a tradition in political economy that was distinctively German in its emphasis upon the historicity of economic institutions and ideas. The line of thought thus begun was continued by Gustav Schmoller and other members of the 'younger' historical school of economics.[16] Weber himself pursued the work of that school into an even further generation and era. Knies was thus a central figure in Weber's background as an economic historian.

Knies's methodological point of departure was a rejection of English classical economic theory.[17] He utterly repudiated what he called "the absolutism of theory," the notion that economic analysis can be

14. Ibid., pp. 451–469, esp. pp. 461–468.

15. Ibid., p. 467.

16. For a sketch of the German historical school of economics, see Ringer, *Decline of the German Mandarins,* pp. 144–147.

17. Knies, *Politische Oekonomie,* esp. pp. 1–35, 70–123, 321–355.

based upon axioms that are independent of time and place. Like economic institutions and practices, he argued, economic theories change and evolve along with their broader historical environment. There can be no exclusively economic field of study, for economic activity cannot be separated from its political, institutional, and cultural settings, which are products of history. The idea that permanent "laws" of economic behavior can be based upon the generality of "private egotism" struck Knies as a pure "fiction," one he rejected on ethical as well as on methodological grounds. By the same token, the pursuit of maximal gain by the greatest possible number seemed to him a false prescription that could have been advanced only where economic affairs were artificially and reprehensibly separated from the ethical and political elements in the life of a people.[18]

Insisting upon the relevance of spiritual forces in history and upon the integration of the economy into the surrounding culture, Knies had recourse to such entities as the collective "organism" and the "character" or "spirit" of a nation. Economic activity, he held, was just one expression of the unified life of a people. The individual economic agent was influenced not only by changeable political and social arrangements but also by his national culture. According to Knies, in fact, the differences of character among peoples were bound to grow with the advance of history. Such traits as industriousness and moderation were developed in divergent degrees by different nations, who were also variously capable of rising ethically above the level of raw egotism. Here Knies assigned an important role to religion. He believed that Christianity had helped to break down obstacles to exchange across tribal and national boundaries, while also fostering habits of industry and thrift. And just as a unity of character could be detected in the actions of individuals, so the collective life of a people was distinctively shaped by a concordance that could not be reduced to private or even collective economic drives.[19]

The historical existence of a people encompasses the various spheres of activity as if from a unified core. And precisely

18. Ibid., pp. 19, 343, 354.
19. Ibid., pp. 79–80, 93–98, 106, 109–110, 114, 343, 355.

because a common spirit permeates all of these, and because everything particular . . . develops in a concordant total movement, a people is something more than a random sum of single individuals.[20]

The passage describes a nation as a kind of individual totality.

Knies sometimes wrote of the "causal" interconnections between economic life and the other elements of a national culture, including the state and the religious institutions. Yet he was clearly uncomfortable with ordinary causal formulations. His problem was that he equated causal connection with "natural necessity," with prediction, and with the universal generalizations of the natural sciences. To him and to other German historians, causal explanation was inherently *"naturgesetzlich"*: it was explanation in terms of laws like those of the natural sciences, or *nomological* explanation in our terms (and Weber's). Since his theoretical commitments and his scholarly practice excluded such explanation from the domain of historical economics, Knies hit upon two fairly plausible substitutes. First, he argued that in his field, the action of causes was not universal, but modified by specific cultural conditions. This accounted for the centrality of "the individual and the concrete" in history. Second, he claimed that "analogies" might be discovered where strict laws could not be found. Incomplete regularities might be detected not only within the several subsections of a culture, and in the way these subsections affected each other, but also in the steps or stages that followed one another in the historical development of nations. Thus both synchronic and diachronic analogies might do for the economic historian what laws did for the natural scientist. The two crucial differences were that analogies held much less strictly than universal regularities, and that they permitted the historian to observe and chart differences as well as similarities in the evolution of nations. Indeed, Knies was chiefly impressed by the differences he observed. He traced the analogies among the various aspects of a nation's history

20. Ibid., p. 109.

to the spirit of its people, and he clearly believed in a plurality of distinctive national characters.[21]

Finally, Knies was deeply concerned with the "freedom" of both individuals and nations to depart from *any* preestablished patterns. Although he considered the individual thoroughly rooted in his culture, he also insisted upon the autonomy of the "personal element" in history. It was this commitment to "human freedom" and the "personal element" that mainly motivated his objection to nomological causality and to economic laws. Even if regular causal connections were found to have obtained in the past, he thought, they did not constrain "free action" in the future. Thus history encompassed a realm of freedom as well as a realm of necessity. The qualities of a nation's territory might restrict its options, as might the established character of its people. Yet necessity and causal regularity in history were always subject to the variability introduced by the personal element. The historical economist was wise to consider the natural constraints upon human choices. Yet especially with the advance of education and morality, he must also do justice to the realm of human freedom.[22]

Knies's works in economic history were still much used in Weber's time, including by Weber himself. The leadership of the 'younger' historical school of economics, however, had by then passed to Gustav Schmoller, who also dominated the famous Social Policy Association (Verein für Sozialpolitik). This was a partly academic and partly public forum for the study and advocacy of moderate social reform. The social policies championed by the association under Schmoller's influence came to strike Weber and a few of his colleagues as problematic. They seemed excessively paternalistic and bureaucratic in tendency; but above all, they rested on ad hoc policy compromises, rather than fully reflected—and explicitly contested—sociocultural objectives. This eventually provoked a debate about value judgments in scholarship in which Weber played a leading part. But even before that debate was launched, Schmol-

---

21. Ibid., pp. 111–116, 339–347, along with notes 17–19, including for the preceding paragraph.

22. Ibid., pp. 334–341, 352.

ler's brand of historical economics was challenged by the Austrian neoclassical economist Carl Menger, one of the initiators of the marginal utility theory that has become a fundament of modern economic analysis.[23] In 1883 Menger published a programmatic tract that set off a bitter and protracted 'methods controversy,' and that clearly affected Weber's later reflections. Menger's central thesis was that economic theory should not be confused—and could not be replaced—*either* by historical accounts of economic practices *or* by the practical policy studies Menger termed "political economy."[24]

In specifying his conception of *theoretical* economics, Menger raised crucial issues, not only for the historical school of economics, but for the German historical tradition as a whole. He began by distinguishing two divergent perspectives upon empirical phenomena.

> Our cognitive interest is directed either at the concrete phenomena in their position in space and time and at their concrete interrelationships, or else . . . at the recurrent patterns in which they appear. The former research direction aims at knowledge of the concrete or, more correctly, the individual, the latter at knowledge of the general.[25]

Applying these definitions to insist upon the divide between theoretical and historical economics, Menger further stipulated that the "types" and "typical relations" or "laws" observable in the empirical world are by no means equally strict or invariant in their application to individual cases. He concluded that the theorist cannot hope to know the types and typical relations of particular phenomena in their "full . . . reality," "their totality and their whole complexity."[26] Rather, theoretical economics must be further subdivided into a "realistic-empirical" and an "exact" branch. The realistic-empirical

23. Ringer, *Decline of the German Mandarins*, pp. 146–154.
24. Menger, *Untersuchungen über die Methode*, esp. pp. 3–59; see p. 10 for "political economy."
25. Ibid., pp. 6–7, and esp. p. 3.
26. Ibid., pp. 17, 25–26, and esp. p. 34.

direction may seek to discern "real types" and "empirical laws"; but these will inevitably be imprecise and subject to exceptions. The exact direction must analyze complex phenomena into more elementary constituents and relationships that *can* be represented in rigorous and invariant types and laws; but these will rarely (if ever) be directly applicable to the empirical world. Thus exact economic theory may posit fully informed, rational, and purely 'economic' agents, and to theorize about their behavior, knowing full well that few (if any) such agents are to be found in real life.[27] In the natural sciences too, as Menger pointed out, empirically observed regularities are usually not exact, while rigorous and universal laws are products of analysis and abstraction. (The ideal gas law really *is* 'ideal,' and the laws of motion typically ignore friction.) A thoughtful reader of Menger could hardly fail to miss the questions his work raised about the fundaments of the German historical tradition. After all, if the distinction between abstract-but-exact and empirical-but-inexact regularities was equally relevant to the natural and the human sciences, then the divide between these two realms might *not be as deep* as many believed—and still believe.

The Threat of 'Positivism'

From the 1880s on, an increasing number of German academics expressed concerns about the place of their institutions and traditions in a changing environment. Delayed industrialization in Germany rapidly produced high concentrations of capital. The old elite of educated notables soon found its influence undermined by the power of the moneyed bourgeoisie on the one hand and the weight of the organized proletariat on the other. Along with a particularly destructive form of 'interest politics,' rapid urbanization and technological change threatened the guiding role of traditional culture and of 'mind' itself. In secondary education, 'realistic' or modern schools contested the primacy of the old classical curriculum, while technical and 'utilitarian' studies gained strength at the university level as well. The ultimate admission of nonclassical secondary

27. Ibid., pp. 35–42.

graduates to higher education, along with the introduction of common elementary schooling during the Weimar period, led to enrollment increases at the universities that accelerated dramatically from the 1870s to the 1920s.

The orthodox majority of the 'German mandarins' met these developments with undisguised hostility. They resisted the 'influx of the masses' into the universities; they condemned the new 'interest politics' and the 'materialism' of the masses, using the 'unpolitical' rhetoric of the 'national cause'; they lamented the decline of 'culture' and the rise of spiritually barren 'civilization.' They saw their time as one of shallow 'utilitarianism,' of social 'dissolution' and moral 'decomposition.' Under the Weimar Republic, which they loathed, many of them preached a 'spiritual revolution' against the new regime and against every aspect of modernity.[28]

A creative minority among German academic intellectuals, including Max Weber, shared some of the concerns of their orthodox colleagues but responded in a more complex and deliberate way. They saw that at least some of the changes taking place were irreversible, and that neither the bureaucratic monarchy nor the official culture of the Wilhelmian era were perfect expressions of the German spirit. If they were to assert a guiding influence upon the newly emerging forces, these 'modernists' reasoned, they would have to adapt their cultural heritage to an inevitably more democratic age. This was an inherently creative stance, for it required a critical clarification of both cognitive and normative commitments. Even tacit assumptions and mute practices had to be converted into explicit methodological prescriptions if a whole intellectual tradition was to be selectively 'translated' for a new context.

These considerations should help to account for the methodological discussions that began during the 1880s, and that encompassed the revitalization of the *Geisteswissenschaften,* the humanistic or interpretive disciplines. Yet the German intellectual field of that time was also characterized by a widespread revulsion against 'positivism,' and against a supposed excess of scholarly specialization.

---

28. For this social and intellectual context, see Ringer, *Decline of the German Mandarins,* esp. pp. 57–59, 73–79, 219–223, 242–250.

Indeed, many felt that the German academic community itself was partly to blame for its declining influence, for it had lost much of what had inspired it during the great decades around 1800. In its heroic age, German *Wissenschaft* had been thoroughly interlinked with the quest for personal *Bildung* and for a meaningful world view *(Weltanschauung)* in the spirit of German Idealism. That connection had found its last great expression in Georg Wilhelm Friedrich Hegel's philosophical system. What followed was a period of increasing specialization, in which *Wissenschaft* eventually came to signify no more than an accumulation of routine research.[29]

Moreover, the period from about 1840 to 1880 saw a great increase in the influence of the natural sciences, both in the academic world and in the broader culture. As the theoretical and practical achievements of the sciences attracted public attention, more or less explicitly scientistic philosophies gained a hearing. During the late 1860s and 1870s, Friedrich Albert Lange and other early neo-Kantians combined a highly positive view of scientific empiricism with a critical emphasis upon the active role of the human subject in the constitution of knowledge. Thus Lange challenged both spiritualist and materialist metaphysics in the name of Kant's critique of speculative reason. Along with a strict phenomenalism, Lange urged a rigorous logical distinction between descriptive and prescriptive propositions, the world of phenomena and the realm of 'the ideal.' Klaus Christian Köhnke has shown how thoroughly the early neo-Kantians identified scientific empiricism, political liberalism, and social progress. He has also documented the extraordinarily abrupt reorientation of German neo-Kantianism between 1878 and 1880, a shift that was plainly motivated by the need for an ideological defense of the existing sociopolitical system.[30] After 1880 and increasingly after 1890, in any case, most German academics lamented the advance of disciplinary specialization, which threatened to separate the search for knowledge from the aspiration to wisdom. At the same time, they became determined opponents of 'positivism.'

29. Ibid., pp. 102–107, 253–258.
30. Lange, *Geschichte des Materialismus,* esp. pp. iii–xiv, 233–557; Köhnke, *Entstehung des Neukantianismus,* esp. pp. 233–432.

Trying to assess the role of 'positivism' in the German intellectual field around the turn of the century, one initially finds it difficult to locate or define the phenomenon with any precision. There were few if any serious disciples of Auguste Comte among German academics. Indeed, to the best of my knowledge, there were no *self-confessed* 'positivists,' at least before the emergence of the Vienna Circle and its neopositivist program during the late 1920s. Those accused of 'positivism' by its numerous critics were therefore presumably guilty of *unacknowledged* fallacies. Chief among these was the belief that the methods of the natural sciences, especially the search for empirical regularities, should be extended to the social and cultural studies as well. Popularizers of scientistic visions and orthodox Marxists were natural suspects. But even unreflected research practices could be considered positivist if they naively envisaged a theory-free accumulation of 'basic facts,' or if they were guided by a strong causalist program, aiming at 'objective' explanations and neglecting 'subjective' or interpretive insights.[31]

Woodruff Smith has described a strand of thought in the German cultural and social sciences that may reasonably be termed 'positivist,' or even 'naturalist.' In his consideration of the period from the 1840s to the 1920s, Smith follows a few selected academics and publicists who were active in fields somewhat removed from the mainstream of interpretive and historical studies on the one hand, and of Idealist philosophy on the other. These men were influenced by such scientist-philosophers as Rudolf Virchow and Wilhelm Ostwald. For the period around the turn of the century, Smith focuses upon the human geographer Friedrich Ratzel, the anthropologist Adolf Bastian, the historian Karl Lamprecht, and above all the psychologist Wilhelm Wundt, undoubtedly the dominant figure within the so-called Leipzig Circle.[32] Wundt was important because he embodied the prestige of the strong psychophysical tradition in German experimental psychology, and he apparently regarded psychology as a foundation for the human and social sciences generally, implying the reducibility of the mental to the psychological or

31. Ibid., pp. 295–301, and pp. 308–309 for the Vienna Circle.
32. Smith, *Politics and the Science of Culture.*

physiological. As we shall see, Weber repudiated not only Wundt's species of psychologism but also Wilhelm Ostwald's scientistic philosophy, which in any case found few converts among German university faculty.

The large majority of German academics outside the natural sciences deeply distrusted scientistic viewpoints that implied a metaphysics of mechanistic determinism or 'materialism.' Indeed, they rejected any mechanical, 'atomistic,' or otherwise reductionist analyses of organic or 'teleological' processes, complex mental states, cultural meanings, or social wholes. During the 1880s and 1890s, the critical project of the early neo-Kantians was superseded by the more 'constructive' neo-Kantianism of the Baden or southwest German school, which was led by Wilhelm Windelband and Heinrich Rickert. Here is how Windelband described the difference between the early, purely 'critical' neo-Kantians and his own later, more 'doctrinal' direction.

> This [early] agnostic neo-Kantianism . . . had a decided bias toward positivism. . . . The empiricist epistemology that was read into Kant . . . confused Kantian a priority with psychic priority [and thus] ended by leaning again toward David Hume on the one hand and toward Auguste Comte on the other. But . . . this had never been . . . intended by Kant: he always saw his 'critical task' . . . as a prelude to 'doctrinal' work. The epistemology that partly identified itself with his name, however . . . [amounted to the] abandonment of all *Weltanschauung* based on *Wissenschaft*. And in this . . . empiricism, a certain naive materialism probably also played a confused and unconscious role.[33]

Though not without meaning, the passage shows how broad the charge of 'positivism' could be. It not only encompassed a critique of naive empiricism; it was also launched in the name of a doctrinal commitment to post-Kantian Idealism. From the 1890s on, in

---

33. See Ringer, *Decline of the German Mandarins,* pp. 305–307, esp. p. 307 for the quote from Windelband, *Die Philosophie im deutschen Geistesleben,* pp. 83–84.

short, 'positivism' figured in the German intellectual field as a major threat to sound scholarship in an age of excessive specialization, and as an obstacle in the path of a sorely needed renewal of Idealism. To the orthodox mandarins, positivism was a kind of intellectual acid, a potentially disastrous dissolvent of holistic concepts, traditional beliefs, and socially integrative certainties.

For German historians, the issues discussed under the heading of 'positivism' became particularly acute during the controversy aroused by the publication of the first volume of Karl Lamprecht's *German History* in 1891. Repudiating the predominant emphasis upon the state and the role of great individuals in the German historical tradition, Lamprecht proposed an integral "cultural history" that gave attention to everything from economic conditions to interpersonal relations and popular culture, while also drawing heavily upon the history of art and architecture. In a 1905 collection of lectures, Lamprecht urged the replacement of narratives organized around "heroes" with comparative analyses of changing "conditions." His early interest in economic history may have earned him the tendentious reproach of "materialism." His mature program for "modern" scientific history, however, was based upon an overarching theory of "psychic differentiation." He saw the individual progressing from an initially total integration into the clan, via looser ties to the community, family, and social group, toward increasing interpersonal differences, individual autonomy, and self-awareness. In a sequence of distinctive "cultural epochs," humanity thus moved from the "symbolic" age, through the "typical" and "conventional" periods, to the modern era of "individualism" and "subjectivism."[34]

Lamprecht was interested in the early anthropologists and sociologists; but his chief methodological commitment was to the psychology of Wilhelm Wundt. He explicitly characterized history as "applied psychology," especially social psychology. While "psychic differentiation" was presumably a singular trend, Lamprecht ob-

34. Now basic on Lamprecht is Chickering, *Karl Lamprecht*. See also Ringer, *Decline of the German Mandarins*, pp. 302–304; Lamprecht, *Moderne Geschichtswissenschaft*.

served regularities in the "psychic mechanisms" of cultural epochs and of the "transitions" between them. As one epoch gave way to its successor—or an earlier to a later phase of "subjectivism," older modes of thought and feeling underwent "dissociation," while a wealth of new stimuli, intruding from the environment, gradually converged in a new psychic "dominant" or "synthesis." Thus the subjectivist era at first entailed an "increase in the activity of the nervous system" and a new "susceptibility to stimuli" *(Reizbarkeit)*. Once fully developed, however, the standpoint of the self-conscious subject permitted the organization of chaotic sensations into formed experience; adapting Kant's usage, Wundt referred to this transformation as one of "apperception."[35]

Lamprecht traced the antecedents of his approach to Herder's idea of a 'people's soul,' to Wilhelm Heinrich Riehl's studies of folk culture, and to Jakob Burckhardt's documentary analysis of art. He apparently believed that these precursors of cultural history could not have given adequate attention to the "social psyche" before the modern individual had begun to emerge. In tracing the second phase of the subjectivist epoch to the stimuli provided by urbanization and rapid technological change, he evoked the psychological pressures of modernity. This allowed him to move on with remarkable ease to the "search for a new dominant," the "yearning of the age" for a new morality, a new *Weltanschauung* or religion, the displacement of artistic naturalism by a new "idealism," and the new primacy of the humanistic disciplines. He promptly detected a general revulsion against "planlessly individualistic research . . . for its own sake," and a demand for a wider analytical perspective. This he found in the "methodological axiom" that the "innermost psychological processes" must be uncovered and "traced back to general laws, whether of psychological mechanics or of an evolutionary psychology or biology." These formulations begin to suggest a reductive psychophysical naturalism.[36]

Roger Chickering has pointed out that Lamprecht's *German History* was riddled with errors and inconsistencies. Reading his

35. Ibid., pp. 1–2, 15–16, 18, 44–45, 49, 56, 62, 65.
36. Ibid., pp. 3–4, 9–14, 48, 62–64, 74–76.

lectures today, moreover, one is struck by the looseness of his evocative descriptions, in which virtually anything could be integrated into a broader 'psychological' dynamic—and thus 'explained' at will. Lamprecht's theoretical apparatus was utterly unfalsifiable and plainly gratuitous in relation to the empirical findings he so effortlessly compounded. In any case, his program struck most of his colleagues as subversive, not only in its methodology but in its social and political implications as well. He was deservedly criticized for his slovenly scholarship, and he was suspected of "economic materialism" even by the usually moderate Friedrich Meinecke. The conservative nationalist historian Georg von Below went a good deal further. Using a range of weapons from the anti-'positivist' arsenal, he associated Lamprecht's approach with Enlightenment rationalism, narrow empiricism, cosmopolitanism, and English historical positivism. He noted that champions of democracy and the masses welcomed cultural history, while more representative historians continued to emphasize the state, the nation, and the holistic concepts developed by the German Romantics.[37] Altogether, Lamprecht found few supporters within the German historical profession. Indeed, it proved so easy to repudiate him as a dilettante and a 'positivist' that he almost certainly retarded the opening to the social sciences that was beginning to transform historical studies in France by the turn of the century.[38]

In 1902 Eduard Meyer, a highly respected and innovative historian of antiquity, wrote a methodological essay that was certainly affected by the Lamprecht controversy, and that later drew a critical response from Weber. Meyer scoffed at the "modern" direction in historiography, which insisted on imitating the natural sciences. He was particularly offended at the equation of history with "applied psychology," the emphasis upon "mass" phenomena, social collectivities, and the "typical" or "general," rather than the "singular" and "individual." What the scientistic historians ignored, according to Meyer, was the "free will" of the human agent and the role of "ideas" in history. In the face of such modern fallacies, Meyer

37. Ringer, *Decline of the German Mandarins,* p. 304.
38. Ringer, *Fields of Knowledge,* pp. 263–282.

reasserted the importance of free action in pursuit of chosen ends, along with the role of "chance" in historical development.[39]

Like Knies before him, Meyer apparently believed that causal relationships between events could only be based upon the natural necessity of deterministic laws. Yet as a practitioner, he found it hard to escape the conviction that "accidents" and deliberate actions *do* shape historical outcomes. Like Knies, he sought to escape this dilemma by means of ad hoc adjustments that were unequally coherent and consistent with each other. Perhaps in history, discoverable regularities were loose "analogies"—that could be affected by the intervention of human agency or of sheer chance. Or, if reality was a vast system of intersecting causal chains, an 'accident' might be defined as a member of a chain not presently under study, a storm during a naval campaign, for example. At the same time, so Meyer believed, the whole antithesis between necessity and contingency could be restated as the difference between a completed and an ongoing sequence of events. Once events have taken place, we must accept them as necessary effects of their antecedents. While matters are still in flux, however, we may consider particular developmental paths as more or less probable, while also acknowledging that consequences we anticipate may be altered by intervening "accidents" or freely chosen actions.[40] Finally, Meyer welcomed Heinrich Rickert's insistence upon the historian's primary interest in the unique and the singular.

In an essay on the emergence of quantum theory during the Weimar period, Paul Forman has noted a "tendency among German physicists and mathematicians to reshape their own ideology" in line with that of their colleagues outside the natural sciences, and actually to join in the widespread "repudiation of positivist conceptions of the nature of science." Indeed, Forman suspects that the "intuitionist" direction in mathematics and the "movement to dispense with causality in physics, which . . . blossomed . . . in Germany after 1918, was primarily an effort by German physicists to adapt the content of their science to the values of their intellectual

39. Meyer, *Zur Theorie und Methodik der Geschichte*, pp. 3–11.
40. Ibid., pp. 13–28.

environment." It is Forman's sense that many 'German mandarins' strenuously repudiated the very idea of causality, which they equated with "suffocating determinism." "If the physicist were to improve his public image," Forman writes, "he had first and foremost to dispense with causality, with rigorous determinism, that most abhorred feature of the physical world picture."[41] The link between causality and determinism was certainly a major factor in the antipositivist reaction that apparently grew in intensity from the 1890s to the early 1930s. German academics outside the natural sciences first began to refer to a "crisis of culture" before the turn of the century; by the interwar period, many also believed in a "crisis of *Wissenschaft*" or of learning. The word "crisis" simultaneously signaled the dangers of 'positivism' and the emergence of a new "idealism" in philosophy and the humanities. By the 1920s, the "philosophy of life" *(Lebensphilosophie)* and the quest for cognitive "synthesis" and intuitive insight led to outright flirtations with irrationalism, at least in some quarters.[42] In its origins during the 1880s and 1890s, however, the renewal of the humanistic disciplines was a substantial and potentially creative enterprise, which we must now consider.

The Revival of the Humanistic Disciplines

In 1883, just as Menger launched his critique of German historical economics, the Berlin philosopher Wilhelm Dilthey published his *Introduction to the Humanistic (or Interpretive) Disciplines (Geist-eswissenschaften)*. His purpose was to codify the concepts and methods of these disciplines, particularly as they contrast with those of the natural sciences. While human beings as psychophysical or biological entities are part of nature, Dilthey held, practitioners of the interpretive disciplines deal essentially with the human mind and spirit *(Geist),* as it has expressed itself in the historical world. They

41. Forman, "Weimar Culture, Causality, and Quantum Theory," pp. 4, 7, 14, 17–18, esp. p. 4.
42. Ringer, *Decline of the German Mandarins,* pp. 245–248, 360–374, 379–389, 392–393, 398–400, 412–417.

do not seek regularities or 'laws'; nor are they intent upon the kind of knowledge that permits the 'mastery' of the environment. Their attention is directed to the unique—and to freely chosen action. While human motives certainly affect historical outcomes, Dilthey argued, they differ radically from other causes of change. Human agency can only be understood 'from the inside,' in terms of intentions and beliefs. The study of anthropology may facilitate the work of interpretation. But the *Geisteswissenschaften* must ultimately be grounded in a "descriptive and analytical psychology" that does not rely on psychophysical laws, or on other reductive or 'explanatory' tactics.[43]

The project Dilthey thus initiated in 1883—and in an 1894 essay on descriptive psychology—did not reach its maturest form until 1907, with his *Construction of the Historical World in the Geisteswissenschaften,* which was further elaborated in subsequent years. In a classic statement of the interpretive position, Dilthey here worked with a threefold scheme of "immediate experience" *(Erleben, Erlebnis),* "Expression" *(Ausdruck),* and "interpretive understanding" *(Verstehen).* He was particularly emphatic about the primacy of immediate awareness. Our 'lived' experience, he stipulated, is an initially unanalyzed complex of present sensations, memories, and anticipations, of perceptions, intentions, and evaluative orientations. The fullness of this vital totality provides the raw material for any observations we may articulate, transform into *organized* experience *(Erfahrung),* and possibly integrate into the cognitive frameworks of the various disciplines. This part of Dilthey's thought inspired what came to be called 'philosophy of life' *(Lebensphilosophie).* It also affected Dilthey's own further reflections in important ways. Above all, Dilthey always believed that *Nacherleben,* the empathetic reproduction of an immediate experience, played a role in the genesis of interpretive understanding. A primitive form of *Verstehen,* he suggested, might be a virtually unconscious—though culturally conditioned—insight

43. Dilthey, *Einleitung in die Geisteswissenschaften,* esp. book I, pp. 3–120; see key passages on pp. 5–6, 9–17, 26–38, 64–68, 90–92, 116. See also Dilthey, "Ideen," pp. 139–240. Dilthey traced the word *Geisteswissenschaften* to John Stuart Mill; Weber noted its use in German by Hermann von Helmholtz in "Knies," p. 44.

into the meaning of gestures, facial expressions, and simple actions.[44]

Yet even while retaining this subjectivist view of empathetic understanding, the mature Dilthey also developed a more complex account of *Verstehen*. To capture the sense of reconstructing human meanings from their manifestations, he loosely adapted the Hegelian terminology of 'objectification.' Texts, artifacts, and institutions of all kinds can be considered externalized or 'objectified' traces of 'mind'; the interpreter's task is to reconstruct the historical world from such objectively available traces. Human understanding can be most easily achieved on the basis of intellectual commonalities, or within a language community; but the languages of other cultures can be learned as well. Among the possible objects of interpretation, Dilthey distinguished the expression of an immediate experience, a purposive human action, and a purely intellectual construction or judgment. Even with respect to immediate experience, he suggested, we seek the 'distanced' articulation of objective knowledge *(Erfahrung)*. Actions, of course, are understood in terms of motives and intentions. The most interesting aspect of Dilthey's late work, however, was his attempt to explicate the interpretation *(Verstehen, Auslegung)* of what he called intellectual "structures" or "patterns of thought." His point was that we can understand such products of mind as legal codes and mathematical theorems by retracing the reasoning on which they are based. The way in which the parts of a text are related to form a coherent whole, too, may be rationally reconstructed with some degree of reliability. As an objectification of mind, Dilthey noted, a text becomes independent of the author's psyche; it is integrated into a set of texts that jointly form an intellectual context or a tradition. The relationship among texts is one of mutual adaptation and influence *(Wirkungszusammenhang)*, which extends over time, right to our own day. For we live in a historical world of inherited meanings.

44. Dilthey, *Aufbau der geschichtlichen Welt,* chs. II ("Der Aufbau . . ."), III ("Plan der Fortsetzung zum Aufbau . . ."), pp. 79–220, esp. pp. 84–88, 130–162, 197, 205–220, including for what follows. See also Ermarth, *Dilthey,* esp. pp. 3–178.

While fascinating in their scope, Dilthey's formulations—and re-formulations—never became fully clear. Perhaps his difficulty stemmed from his overriding commitment to the separation of the humanistic studies from the natural sciences. He continued to see psychophysical man as a part of nature, while also conceding the impact of natural processes upon the choices open to historical agents. Nevertheless, he contrasted the 'freedom' of the human mind with the lawfulness of nature. Indeed, he identified causal relationships with nomological *(naturwissenschaftlich)* laws and with necessity, which made him all the more anxious to dissociate intellectual influence from causal connection.[45] History is "immanently teleological," he wrote; human purposes and values are realized in the network of meanings and intellectual influences that make up the historical world. *Verstehen* provides access to the 'inner' connections within that world, which further distinguishes the humanities from the natural sciences. The historian is interested not in regularities, but in individualities, including distinctive cultures, national spirits, and epochs defined by great individuals. Finally, Dilthey never lost his conviction that empathy is an element in interpretation. *Verstehen,* he wrote, always contains "something irrational."

Some of the positions Dilthey thus fully articulated after the turn of the century were actually anticipated by the sociologist and philosopher Georg Simmel as early as 1892, even before Dilthey developed his case for a descriptive psychology. This is important, though often overlooked, because Simmel ultimately influenced Weber much more directly than Dilthey did. Simmel's short treatise on *Problems in the Philosophy of History* itself was revised and expanded in 1905, perhaps partly in response to further analyses by the philosophers Wilhelm Windelband in 1894 and Heinrich Rickert in 1896 and 1902. Yet in all essentials, Simmel's argument was complete by 1892. Like Dilthey, Simmel focused upon the relationship between inner "movements" of the "soul" and their outward expressions. In all human interactions, he noted, we presuppose mental states in others; we infer their thoughts and feelings from

45. See esp. Dilthey, *Aufbau,* p. 197.

their actions and gestures, reasoning from visible "effects" to inner "causes." Asking how historians achieve their understanding *(Verstehen)* of past human behaviors and beliefs, Simmel assigned a special place to the "theoretical contents of thought," which can be reconstructed independently of the intentions of their originators. Obviously, much greater difficulties arise in the understanding of subjective states. Interpreters may never fully grasp emotions beyond their own prior experience, Simmel believed; but *some* degree of insight is apparently possible even with respect to largely unfamiliar feelings. While insisting that we can know human history in a way that we cannot know nature, Simmel firmly rejected the notion of understanding as a kind of telepathic reproduction. The historian's ability at least partly to identify with others, he argued, is not a fact but a heuristic assumption, one that allows us to begin the process of interpretation at all. In the end, Simmel was prepared to admit that our methods of *Verstehen* are still something of a mystery to us.[46]

In a particularly interesting chapter, Simmel addressed the issue of "laws in history." Following Hume, he defined a law as the assertion that the occurrence of a set of facts is invariably followed by certain consequences. But in the world we know, he continued, many processes converge at particular times and places, and the events we observe succeeding each other are extremely complex. We cannot judge whether they are lawfully linked, unless we first analyze them into their component elements. Thus we can conclude in favor of an invariant connection between an element (a) in a total state {a, b, c} and an element (a1) in a total state {a1, b1, c1} only if the element (a) is followed by (a1) even in such different total states as {a, d, e} and {a1, d1, e1}. Simmel further argued (1) that we cannot expect to analyze a complex state into *all* its elementary constituents, and (2) that such complex states will almost certainly not recur with exactly similar components. A fully lawful connection between two historical events *as totalities* is therefore effectively impossible.

---

46. Simmel, *Probleme der Geschichtsphilosophie,* pp. 1–33, esp. pp. 1, 4–6, 14–17, 20–21. Citations are from the 1892 edition, although Weber sometimes cites the second edition of 1905.

Simmel's purpose, clearly, was to undermine the vision of history as a sum of strictly deterministic regularities. He saw scientific laws as 'ideal,' and thus different *in logic* from descriptions of particular events. History, he wrote, is not a *"Gesetzeswissenschaft,"* a nomological science, but a *"Wirklichkeitswissenschaft,"* a discipline concerned with concrete realities. The borderline between these two kinds of inquiries did not seem to him unbridgeable; but he insisted that historical knowledge is of great human interest quite independently of the scientific search for universal regularities.[47]

Having effectively excluded invariant laws in history, Simmel was prepared to recommend recourse to more loosely conceived 'laws.' By way of example, he cited such statistical regularities as suicide rates in given societies. He observed that we can arrive at rough generalities about such phenomena without knowing much about the particulars they aggregate. He also mentioned the 'law' of 'differentiation,' which asserts a generally increasing specialization of functions and traits among human beings through the ages. Imperfect laws, he argued, should be expected to conflict on occasion; but they are nonetheless useful in the organization of data, in the identification of "typical" developments or relationships, and as preliminary steps toward more exact knowledge. One is reminded of Menger's distinction between abstract-but-exact and empirical-but-inexact regularities. But Simmel drew an even sharper line between all empirical approaches to history, and inquiries into its 'meaning' or 'purpose.' Perfect knowledge of all historical processes, he observed, would still fail to reveal their ultimate significance. Whether historical change adds up to "progress," for example, can only be decided on the basis of extra-historical judgments. Nevertheless, historical studies *must* be guided by concerns about the human significance of the issues taken up, for the complex realities of the past cannot simply be enumerated. Historians must have questions to put to their data.[48]

Weber owed much to Simmel; but he also benefited from a new line of analysis that began with Wilhelm Windelband's famous

47. Ibid., pp. 34–70, esp. pp. 34–44, 54–56, 60, 64–65 (43 for *"Wirklichkeitswissenschaft"*).

48. Ibid., pp. 71–109, esp. pp. 71–72, 81–84, 92.

rectoral address of 1894 on "History and the Natural Sciences." Windelband's ideas were subsequently refined and elaborated by Heinrich Rickert, a younger member of the Baden or southwest German school of neo-Kantians. Windelband opened his case by assigning to philosophy the task of logically clarifying the concepts of the specialized disciplines. By way of example, he criticized the conventional division of the empirical studies into the natural sciences and the humanistic disciplines. He observed that this divide was based upon the "material" or substantive difference between 'nature' and 'mind' as subject matters; but he instanced psychology to show that the separation was sometimes hard to maintain. In its place, he proposed a "formal" or methodological distinction. The empirical disciplines usually identified as humanistic, interpretive, or historical, he argued, seek "fully and exhaustively" to describe a "single, more or less extended event" at a particular location in time. The "cognitive purpose" of these disciplines is to "reproduce and understand" a "form of human life" in its "unique actuality." Methodologically, the empirical disciplines in fact fall into two groups: the *Gesetzeswissenschaften* pursue "nomothetic" knowledge of the general in the form of invariant "laws"; the *Ereigniswissenschaften* strive for "idiographic" knowledge of singular patterns or events. Windelband held that the same set of phenomena can be studied in both the nomothetic and the idiographic mode, and that the borderline between the two approaches is not absolute. Even organic nature as we know it can be both nomothetically systematized and considered a singular development not likely to be repeated on other planets.[49]

In the context of a partly ceremonial lecture, Windelband richly elaborated the difference between the two types of knowledge. He pictured historians bringing back to life the persons and events of the past in their full "individuality" and "immediacy" *(Anschaulichkeit)*. From the mass of their source materials, he continued, they try to extract "images" of human lives in the "whole wealth of their distinctive forms." The natural sciences, by contrast,

49. Windelband, "Geschichte und Naturwissenschaft," in *Präludien*, pp. 355–379, esp. pp. 357, 361–364.

deal in "abstractions"; they give us a "world of atoms" that is "colorless," devoid of all "sensuous qualities," a "triumph of thought over perception." The application of "positivist" principles to human affairs yields no more than a few trivial generalities. Nomothetic laws do offer us a chance to intervene in the world. But the cultural life of humanity is an ever richer fabric of historical connections, and we can participate in it only if we understand its development. In any case, empirical particulars are *not* of interest only to the extent that they can be subsumed under general laws, but also if they form significant components of a vital "totality" *(Gesamtanschauung)*. At any rate, Windelband insisted, our deepest concerns and commitments direct our attention toward "the singular and the unique"; "all our value orientations are grounded in the . . . incomparability of our subject. . . . That is proven above all by our relationship to the (great) personalities."[50]

Windelband conceded that historical explanation depends in principle upon nomothetic laws, especially the laws of psychology. In practice, to be sure, historians rely mainly upon their informal insight into human nature, their "tact" and "intuition." Above all, as Windelband insisted, nomothetic knowledge can never really account for the distinctive patterns of real events: "[For] in causal analysis, every particular event takes the form of a syllogism, in which the major premise is a scientific law, or a number of lawful necessities, the minor premise is a condition given in time, or a complex of such conditions, and the conclusion is the actual singular event." Thus sets of conditions always figure among the antecedents of subsequent events, and the total state of the world can be deduced only from the *conjunction* of its prior state and the laws of change. For Windelband, it followed that the historically and individually given always contains a remnant of the "ineffable" and "undefinable." The "innermost essence of the human personality," for example, "resists analysis into general categories." We experience its final "incomprehensibility" as "causelessness" and "individual freedom." In any case, laws and events remain ultimately incommensurate objects of knowledge.[51]

50. Ibid., pp. 369–374.
51. Ibid., pp. 375–378.

As a theoretician of the German historical tradition, Windelband shifted the focus from what I have called the *principle of empathy* to the *principle of individuality*. He virtually ignored not only 'nomothetic' psychology but Dilthey's reflections upon the humanistic disciplines as well. As we shall see, Weber himself firmly opposed attempts to reduce the study of human affairs to the search for psychophysical regularities, which he considered forms of 'naturalism' or 'psychologism.' Moreover, he showed little sustained interest in Dilthey's 'descriptive' psychology or in his account of empathetic 'reexperiencing.' To be sure, Weber's methodological position was formed before Dilthey's most interesting work was published. It is widely believed that Weber extended the interpretive theories of Wilhelm Dilthey, and in a very broad sense, this view is not unreasonable. Nevertheless, Weber certainly learned less from Dilthey than from Simmel. Indeed, while Windelband's vision of 'idiographic' knowledge certainly interested Weber, it also raised difficulties that Simmel had largely avoided. Two years before Windelband's address, Simmel had distinguished the nomological sciences *(Gesetzeswissenschaften)* from the disciplines concerned with concrete reality *(Wirklichkeitswissenschaften)*. Moreover, he had recognized the 'ideal' character of strictly universal generalizations, the possible uses of statistical regularities, and the impossibility of explaining particular events *as totalities*.

Simmel had thus protected himself against the most serious flaw in Windelband's position, which was precisely his tendency to treat idiographic particulars as totalities. What can it mean to say, after all, that the historian must 'fully and exhaustively' describe an event, to 'reproduce and understand' a human situation in its 'unique actuality,' 'individuality,' or 'immediacy'? How can a given fact be said to be significant as an element in a 'totality'?—The 'conclusion' of a syllogism in which laws and conditions figure as major and minor premises surely cannot be an 'actual singular event,' but only an event as defined or described in a certain way. For one can never *exhaustively* describe or explain an event or a state of the world. To discuss an event at all—or to point up its 'uniqueness,' we must first characterize it in a way that picks out the aspects or features that interest us—or that we want to contrast or explain. This may be called the *problem of description*. Elaborating upon Windelband's essay of 1894, Heinrich Rickert took up this problem, along with related issues, in his 1902 *Limits of Scientific Conceptualization*.[52] Rickert's difficult and occasionally elusive work—and the way in which Weber adapted it to his own uses—will be our subject in the next chapter.

52. Rickert, *Grenzen der naturwissenschaftlichen Begriffsbildung*. Citations will be from the first complete edition of 1902, although the first three chapters of the book were initially published in 1896.

WEBER'S ADAPTATION OF RICKERT

2

Max Weber read Rickert's *Limits of Scientific Conceptualization* soon after its publication in 1902, as he reported in a letter to his wife: "I have finished Rickert. He is *very* good; in large part I find in him the thoughts I have had myself, though not in logically finished form. I have reservations about his terminology."[1] These sentences are sometimes taken to show that Weber closely followed Rickert in his methodological views. Yet the passage also refers to Weber's own prior reflections, as well as to reservations he considers terminological. This leaves room for divergent interpretations. In any case, the best way to assess Weber's intellectual debt to Rickert is at least briefly to take up the two men's relevant arguments.

Rickert's Position and Its Problems

According to Rickert, the world is an infinitely extensive set of objects, each of which is infinitely subdivisible, so that we confront an 'extensively' as well as 'intensively' infinite 'manifold' of particulars. Obviously, our knowledge cannot be anything like a copy or a reproduction of reality; indeed, we cannot know any object or event in all of its aspects. To comprehend reality is thus conceptually to simplify and to transform it in the light of a cognitive strategy. The strategy of

---

1. Marianne Weber, *Max Weber: A Biography,* trans. H. Zohn (New York: Wiley, 1975), p. 260.

the natural sciences is to analyze objects into their simpler components, trying to arrive at elementary constituents, while also subsum-
ing selected aspects of reality under universal generalization or 'laws'
that hold independently of time and place. The most successful sciences work not only with elementary particles but, even more typically, with such deterministic generalizations as the laws of
mechanics, which deal with relationships rather than with 'things.'
The *disadvantage*—or limitation—of scientific conceptualization, in
Rickert's view, is that it leaves behind the immediate concreteness
(Anschaulichkeit) of ordinary experience in order to achieve the coherence embodied in its hierarchy of invariant laws: "We can immediately experience reality; but . . . as soon as we try to grasp it by means
of the natural sciences, we always lose exactly what makes it reality."
For Rickert, it followed that the infinite manifold of reality may also
be approached with a cognitive strategy *other* than that of the natural
sciences.[2] Like Windelband before him, Rickert found fault with the
traditional division of the academic specialties into the natural sciences and the humanistic disciplines *(Geisteswissenschaften)*. In a tradition begun by Hegel and revitalized by Dilthey and others, the
Geisteswissenschaften were held to deal *interpretively* with the world of
'mind.' Rickert did not object to this usage, which he thought would
endure in practice. What he opposed, however, was a substantive or
ontological divide between the realms of physical nature *(Natur)* and
of the mental or psychic *(Geist, Psyche)*. Instead, expanding Windelband's antithesis between 'nomothetic' and 'idiographic' knowledge,
he recommended a logical distinction between the disciplines search-
ing for universal scientific *(naturgesetzlich)* laws and those interested
in the 'individual' or singular. The flaw in the traditional divide was
exposed by the anomaly of psychology, which could be pursued from
both the perspective of the natural sciences and that of the humanistic
disciplines. According to Rickert, Dilthey was misled into a hopeless
quest for an immediate knowledge of the psychic, in which the
inescapable gap between the inquiring subject and the subject of
inquiry was imagined away. In the meantime, at least partly successful
work was being done in the species of psychology that Dilthey rightly

2. Rickert, *Grenzen*, pp. 33–146, 228–248; p. 238 for quote.

rejected as a basis for the *Geisteswissenschaften*. The search for psycho-physical laws was well under way, and so was the attempt to identify such simple constituents of psychophysical processes as sensations and associations. The only consistent division of the cognitive realm, in short, was that between the generalizing sciences and the disciplines concerned with historically given particulars or 'individuals.'[3]

To designate the main alternative to the natural sciences, Rickert used the term 'history' *(Geschichtswissenschaft)*; but he specifically meant the history of particular objects and events, of "concrete and individual configurations." History, in Rickert's view, is concerned with what occurred at specific times and places, with the singular and unique, with personal as well as collective 'individuals,' and with human beings, events, and objects that have proper names.

> All empirical reality . . . becomes nature when we consider it with regard to the general; it becomes history when we consider it with regard to the particular. Every discipline has its point of departure in immediately experienced reality.

The last sentence is important, for it reaffirms that reality itself cannot be reproduced. To illustrate the point, Rickert commented upon the widely held view that the great individuals resist generalization. According to Rickert, this is true simply because they are real. Thus it is wrong to isolate the great personalities as 'irrational' elements in the historical process. One has to recognize, rather, that all of reality is 'irrational' in the sense that it cannot be encompassed by our concepts. Nevertheless, Rickert clearly believed that history comes much closer than the natural sciences to conveying the fullness of our ordinary relationship to the world. In that sense, history is what Simmel said it was: a discipline dealing with reality *(Wirklichkeitswissenschaft)*.[4]

3. Ibid., pp. 147–225.
4. Ibid., pp. 248–264, esp. pp. 250, 255, 258–260. The reader will recall that Windelband had distinguished 'nomothetic' sciences from 'idiographic' disciplines dealing with events *(Ereigniswissenschaften)*; but the contrast between law-seeking *Gesetzeswissenschaften* and *Wirklichkeitswissenschaften* had first been suggested by Simmel.

Of course, as Rickert conceded, the methodological divide between the natural sciences and the historical disciplines is not absolute. Elements of history—and singular developments—can be found in biology, in evolutionary theory, in geology, and even in astronomy. Conversely, historians often use at least limited generalizations, or what Rickert called 'relatively historical' concepts. In sociology, even social life is approached with the aim of formulating significant generalizations. Yet as Rickert insisted, even relatively historical concepts always serve the historian's principal interest in the unique, and the more sociology models itself upon the natural sciences, the less its findings apply to historical realities. More important, it is only the 'relatively historical' that lends itself to scientific conceptualization, never the great historical personalities, for example. Ignoring his own recurrent warnings against a tempting simplification, Rickert identified the "absolutely historical" with "reality itself"; but this was presumably a rhetorical exaggeration.[5]

Unable fully to reproduce reality, in fact, history can treat only small segments of it, segments that are significant in their singularity. Many of the 'individuals' of interest to the historian have proper names, as Rickert pointed out; but since none can be totally described, general terms are required to characterize them. Thus the historical 'individual' is a construct, not a concrete person, object, or collectivity; but the general terms used to represent it are meant to point up its distinctive qualities, rather than those of its traits that lend themselves to generalization. The only way to conceive a 'historical individual,' according to Rickert, is by means of a necessarily evaluative assessment of the cultural *significance* of that singular person, object, or event. (Historians of modern Germany are interested in the fact that Frederick William IV refused the crown offered him by the Frankfurt Parliament; they do not care who made his coats.) Historical concepts may thus be termed 'teleological'; for they define the 'individual' in the light of certain values. Most of the objects of historical study encompass mental events, or the interaction between mental and physical processes, which partly justifies the term *Geisteswissenschaften*. Yet the central role played by cultural

5. Ibid., pp. 264–304, esp. p. 295.

values and culturally significant 'historical individuals' suggests that the alternative to the natural sciences is more appropriately named the 'historical study of culture' *(historische Kulturwissenschaft)*, or simply history.[6]

While mainly concerned with the particular, the historian must also search for causes, for the world is an infinitely complex network of singular causal connections. Having said that, however, Rickert strenuously dissociated the interrelationships among 'historical individuals' from the necessary connections implied by deterministic laws. On occasion, he actually *equated* "causal explanation" with "nomological *(naturwissenschaftlich)* explanation," which "expresses a 'necessary' connection . . . a law . . . of absolutely universal validity." But his main point was that the mutual influences among historical individualities are neither necessary nor deducible from invariant laws. Like earlier theoreticians of the German historical tradition, he fled the specter of determinism, leaving himself the problem of articulating an alternate model of singular causal explanation. But he never really succeeded in this task. He had no trouble excluding the search for nomological laws as a *goal* of historical inquiry. He was also able to distinguish the concept of 'causal law' from what he termed the 'causal principle,' the Kantian account of causality as a presupposition of all empirical knowledge. But this distinction cannot help the historian to identify particular causal connections. At one point, Rickert cited the sound made by a table when hit, presumably to suggest that certain causal connections may be directly perceived. Possibly echoing Simmel, he further supposed that insight into the link between two events can be derived from the knowledge that some of their constituents are lawfully related. As a last resort, he even conceded that *some* singular causal claims may be deduced from causal laws. But this undercut his earlier arguments, leaving him to repeat merely that the search for regularities is not the historian's main concern.[7]

Rickert himself, meantime, was mainly concerned with the problem of values. To begin with, he distinguished value judgments from

6. Ibid., pp. 305–339, esp. pp. 309–310, 325–326, 339.
7. Ibid., pp. 128–129, 307–308, 409–436, 706–736, esp. p. 129.

judgments of value relatedness. Without making value judgments in their own behalf, he argued, historians may judge certain 'individuals' to be culturally relevant or value related—or actually construct them with a view to their relationship to cultural values. Thus two researchers may differ in their values and yet agree that some singular object or issue is culturally significant. Of course such agreement in turn depends upon *some* shared values, which tends to undermine Rickert's distinction. At any rate, as Rickert argued, the values involved in the historian's judgments must be general in some sense. But values are evolved by human beings living in communities; they are cultural values. Thus values may be empirically general in two ways: they may be commonly accepted as valid either in the historians' own cultures or in the cultures they choose to investigate. Rickert wrote of intellectual 'centers,' human beings of the past whose commitments and 'volitions' help historians to orient their accounts of given eras and to select the particulars to be included in them. Finally, Rickert suggested that values can be considered normatively general if they *ought* to be recognized as such by all educated persons within a culture.[8]

Unfortunately, several of Rickert's formulations do not stand up to close examination. On the one hand, he offered a valuable distinction between 'primary' and 'secondary' historical 'individuals.' 'Primary historical individuals' derive their significance directly from their relationship to cultural values, whereas 'secondary historical individuals,' though not value related, are *causally* relevant to 'primary historical individuals' or 'intellectual centers.' Rickert further pointed out that causal interconnections branch off from any singular configuration in such numerous and endless chains that causal analysis too must be delimited in the light of cultural values.[9] On the other hand, as noted, Rickert's judgments of value relatedness do not remove the need for underlying value judgments. Moreover, the distinction between values held in the historians' own cultures and those held in the cultures they study is problematic, because it fails to specify how the commitments and 'volitions'

8. Ibid., pp. 356–372, 389–390, 560–588.
9. Ibid., pp. 474–480.

of past 'intellectual centers' are known to the historian. Rickert here either tacitly accepted the view that the past can be directly understood 'in its own terms'; or he forgot that the 'intellectual centers' he mentioned must first be selected—or constructed—as significant in the light of the historians' own values. Nor is it clear that every historian writing within a given culture will share all the values prevalent in that culture; beliefs in such matters are rarely homogeneous, which raises questions even about the empirical 'generality' of value commitments in the historian's own environment. Even more damaging, finally, is Rickert's tendency to confound values that are shared in fact with values that *ought* to be respected by educated members of a cultural group. The grounds for such obligatory commitments would have to be specified, and could only lie in the absolute validity of the values involved.

These problems are particularly serious because Rickert equated the *objectivity of historical accounts* with the *general validity of the values* that guide them. Historians attain the highest possible degree of "objectivity," he argued at one point, if their judgments of significance are informed by values that are empirically valid, being generally accepted by a certain circle of persons. What remains in doubt is only their *unconditionally* general validity, the counterpart in the historical disciplines of unconditionally universal truths in the sciences. While acknowledging that the absolute validity of cultural norms cannot currently be demonstrated, Rickert suggested that on a 'supra-empirical plane,' they may be posited as orienting *ideals* in the individualizing disciplines. Thus historical accounts will change, along with the empirical values of the historians' cultures; but they may nevertheless converge, along with the universal history of human culture, toward some unified set of transcendent values. The standpoint from which Rickert advanced these speculative claims was that of a transcendental subjectivism, in which the supra-individual subject was a valuing as well as a knowing one. He repeatedly emphasized that truth itself has to be posited as an unconditional value in the realm of science and learning.[10]

10. Ibid., pp. 631–642, 660–694, esp. p. 631.

Rickert's work was an element in the Baden neo-Kantians' project for a philosophical 'theory of value.' Even more broadly, it was a product of the crisis in German academic culture. As Rickert indicated in his introduction, he meant to counter the threat of positivism and to aid the revival of idealism. Thoughtless specialization and the impact of scientific models, he believed, had left a deficit in the realm of personal *Bildung*. By once again extending philosophy beyond the narrow field of epistemology, he hoped to contribute to the recovery of a theoretically grounded *Weltanschauung*. While he claimed that his methodological remarks were as pertinent to economic history as to the old Rankean historiography, moreover, he repeatedly attacked the emphasis of some historians upon "typical" or "mass phenomena." Against these aberrations, he persistently championed the historical significance of "great men," chiefly Goethe and Bismarck. He even managed a glancing blow against the new "sociology" as an "impoverishment" of *Wissenschaft*.[11]

Like Windelband, Rickert virtually ignored the problem of interpretation. Indeed, this may help to explain his tacit assumption that historians can be guided by the values of the cultures they study. He apparently failed to consider Simmel's early suggestions on this subject, while the mature work of Dilthey was not yet available to him. When he wrote about interpretation at all, at any rate, he restated the most crudely subjectivist account of "understanding" as a "reexperiencing" or an "empathetic identification" *(Nacherleben, Hineinleben, Hineinfühlen)*. Historians as writers, he suggested, should evoke the concrete fullness of reality, bringing the past back to life, so that their readers may reexperience it. When dealing with Goethe or Bismarck, for example, narrators should include personal traits even when these are not directly relevant, so as to capture the vitality of lived experience.[12]

Again like Windelband, Rickert was primarily a theoretician of 'individuality,' rather than of interpretation. At least in principle, he used the term 'individual' *(Individuum)* to designate not only persons but also singular objects and events. At the same time, he

11. Ibid., pp. 7, 10–14, 18–22, 332, 360–361, 595.
12. Ibid., pp. 383, 385, 540–543.

regarded every individuality as utterly unique—and as culturally significant precisely in its uniqueness. In following out this perspective, he ultimately insisted upon the indivisibility of what he called the 'in-dividual' *(In-dividuum)*. By way of example, he cited the name of a famous diamond, which was clearly most valuable in its undivided state. He also compared the relationship between Goethe and an ordinary person to that between the famous diamond and a piece of coal. He did not explain how the physical division of a diamond resembled the conceptual analysis of a person, whose several traits might be unequally relevant to a particular historical account. Perhaps he never fully dispelled the illusion of a fully reproducible reality, at least when it came to great personalities. A "thing" is divisible, he suggested, a "soul" is not.[13]

Extending the metaphor of individuality, Rickert urged that historical development be conceived neither as ordinary change nor as progress, but as a movement through unique stages that is value related not only in its elements, but also as a whole. Historical ages and groups, too, are unique and 'teleologically' significant constellations of unique particulars. Rickert contrasted this holistic approach with the "atomizing individualism" of the Enlightenment, in which society might appear a mere aggregate of identical members—and thus ultimately a "mass phenomenon." The historical whole, he argued, is more than the sums of its parts; it is their "essence" *(Inbegriff)*. Luther was German, but not as a member of the class of Germans. Rather, he helped to define the ideal of the 'German,' which was further enriched by Goethe and Bismarck. Thus the concept 'Germans' does not refer to an average, but takes its meaning from the unique characteristics of great individuals. And in the same way, a cultural milieu or the spirit of an age is shaped by the leading minds, whose insights only gradually penetrate "the masses."[14] If Weber learned anything from Rickert, which remains to be seen, it was surely not this crude historical idealism.

13. Ibid., pp. 342–352, 357–358.
14. Ibid., pp. 307–308, 393–395, 398–400, 405–406, 436–474, 482–484, 496–500.

Weber's Adaptation

Weber wrote his methodological essays explicitly as a reflective practitioner of the cultural and social sciences *(Wissenschaften)*, not as a philosopher. Disavowing any interest in epistemological questions, he proposed more generally to leave all technically philosophical issues to the trained 'logicians,' chiefly Simmel, Windelband, and Rickert. Although he ended by criticizing certain theories advanced by Eduard Meyer, the distinguished historian of antiquity, he joined Meyer in urging his readers not to overestimate the significance of methodological analysis. While it might protect them against loosely 'philosophical' speculations of a certain type, it certainly could not take the place of serious substantive work. An increased interest in methodology becomes understandable and legitimate only when changes occur in the concerns and perspectives that inspire research in the historical and social studies. Such changes may at first lead only to new questions being asked and new sources consulted; but they will eventually raise deeper conceptual problems as well. Clearly, Weber believed that the tensions in his own intellectual field were serious enough to explain and justify his practitioner's interest in methodological issues.[15]

Just as clearly, Weber followed Rickert in the overall framework of his own position. Like Rickert, he rejected the division of the empirical disciplines according to their objects, along the boundary between the physical and the psychic, or 'nature' and 'mind.' More consistent than Rickert in this respect, he avoided the temptation to define the humanistic disciplines in radical opposition to the natural sciences. Still, the starting point of his methodological reflections was Rickert's characterization of reality as an extensively and intensively infinite manifold of objects and events 'within' and 'outside' us. Since our knowledge cannot be anything like a total reproduction of that manifold, we need deliberate strategies of simplification or selection. In Simmel's terminology, Weber distinguished the nomological sciences *(Gesetzeswissenschaften)* from the disciplines dealing with reality *(Wirklichkeitswissenschaften)*. The former disciplines abstract from

15. Weber, "Objektivität," p. 146, note 1; "Studien," pp. 215–218.

the concreteness of ordinary experience in search of causal laws; what is significant or worth knowing in these disciplines is what can be subsumed under class concepts. The laws sought are universal in scope—and correspondingly low in concrete content. Weber suspected even members of the German historical school of believing that reality can be fully deduced from a system of universal laws. But this must be false, for there is a gap between the abstraction of the laws and the concreteness of reality. In fact any singular constellation of particular circumstances can only be traced to the preceding constellation, as Simmel had recognized. In history and in the cultural studies *(Kulturwissenschaften)*, including the social sciences *(Sozialwissenschaften)*, according to Weber, the reduction of events to laws is largely irrelevant, *not* because change is less lawful in this domain than in nature, but because knowledge of social laws is not knowledge of social reality, and what is significant about social reality depends primarily upon our cognitive interests.[16]

The *Wirklichkeitswissenschaften*, including history and the cultural sciences, seek knowledge of reality in its qualitative particularity and uniqueness. They deal with a small fraction of the world's objects and events, namely those that are significant and worth knowing precisely in their distinctiveness. Weber noted that some historians apparently aim at a concept-free description of the entire past. But such a project can only yield an endless list of unconnected propositions; for the elements of the infinite manifold cannot be exhaustively enumerated. We must construct concepts that selectively organize reality, 'isolating' descriptions that pick out what is significant in the light of our concerns. For even Rickert's 'individuals' cannot enter historical accounts as totalities, but only in certain of their traits. The concepts that figure in the 'sciences of reality' do not focus upon what can be subsumed under class concepts, but upon what is distinctive. To know history is thus to know neither timeless laws nor the past as a whole; it is to know what is significant and worth knowing about the past in its characteristic individuality.[17]

16. Weber, "Roscher," pp. 3–5, 12–13; "Objektivität," pp. 171–172, 180; "Stammler," pp. 321–322.

17. Weber, "Roscher," pp. 5–6, 14; "Objektivität," pp. 170–171, 177–178; "Studien," pp. 230–232, 239–240.

Moreover, we want to understand the significant 'individuals' of the past as parts of a universal network of singular causal connections. Particular links in this network are themselves concrete, rather than general, and some of them involve interpretable human actions as causes or effects. In such cases, our need for causal understanding is not satisfied by evidence of recurrent sequences of behavior; we want to grasp the meaning, 'point,' or sense *(Sinn)* of an action. So we must interpret in order to explain. In any case, the particular causal connections that interest us are not usually instances of causal laws. Weber observed that many historians automatically equated causality with lawfulness, and often with determinism as well; he cited Schmoller and Below as examples. In opposition to this view, Weber insisted upon the historian's predominant interest in *singular* causal analysis, in which particular historical outcomes are explained in terms of specific causal antecedents. Indeed, following Rickert, Weber distinguished 'primary' historical facts, which are significant in their own right, from 'secondary' historical facts, which figure among the causes of primary facts. In response to certain examples provided by Meyer, Weber further acknowledged that historians are often concerned with particulars that serve as clues to broadly prevalent conditions, shared beliefs, or patterns of action. Nevertheless, he rejected Meyer's inclusive definition of the historical as the causally effective; for the causal connections of the past too are infinitely numerous, and many historical outcomes are plainly trivial. Therefore, no matter what heuristic *means* historians or students of culture may draw upon, they still need judgments of significance to identify the individual outcomes they seek to explain. In these formulations, Weber clearly continued to pursue Rickert's lead.[18]

Yet Weber did not take the divide between the 'sciences of law' and the 'sciences of reality' quite as seriously as Rickert did. He regarded the distinction as an important theoretical clarification, but he was also aware of its limitations in practice. Early in his critique of Meyer, he proposed to *begin* by discussing the historian's typical

18. Weber, "Roscher," pp. 8–9, 23; "Studien," pp. 233–244, 257–261. Weber's critique of Meyer was less sympathetic than it might have been; for Meyer had conceived past as well as contemporary outcomes as explananda. Still, Weber rightly pointed to the ultimate need for extra-historical judgments of significance.

emphasis upon particular events, but then to take up the use of rules and laws in the study of society as well. As we already noted, he knew that singular historical facts can be significant as symptoms or instances of more general conditions. In the same vein, he explicitly stipulated that the cultural sciences *are* sometimes concerned with mass phenomena of a partly lawful type. He saw laws and observed regularities as cognitive *means* in the historical and cultural disciplines, even while insisting that the *aim* of these disciplines is to understand objects and events that are significant in their individuality. Indeed, statements to this general effect can be found in Rickert's writings as well; but they are given comparatively more weight in Weber's essays, simply because Weber wrote with a view to the practice of historical and social analysis.[19]

Revealing differences of emphasis also separated Weber's from Rickert's account of value judgments in the cultural and social sciences. Weber certainly accepted Rickert's overall view that more or less conscious judgments of significance guide historians in the choice of their objects of study. To investigate the cultural world is to select from the infinite manifold of reality in the light of human interests: "Culture is a finite segment of the senseless infinitude of the world process that has been invested with meaning and significance from a human point of view." The imputation of cultural significance is a *presupposition,* not a result, of research in this domain; Weber never wavered from that position. But again he weakened or ignored some of the technicalities of Rickert's theory. Thus Rickert had tried to sustain an inherently problematic distinction between judgments of 'value relatedness' and outright value judgments, whereas Weber largely equated the two. Rickert had argued that the values inspiring historians might be 'empirically general' *either* in their own cultures *or* in those they investigated, without specifying how the beliefs of other cultures could be established in advance of any research. Weber gave much thought to the problem of understanding other cultures, but he left no doubt that the normative commitments guiding social scientists are necessarily their own. He saw that scholars will want to work on topics that

19. Weber, "Objektivität," pp. 176–179; "Studien," p. 216.

seem to them of universal significance, and that their relevant preferences will tend to reflect those of their intellectual environment. Yet he acknowledged that their interests might be partly personal as well. He thus bracketed several of Rickert's complexities, and concluded simply that work in the cultural sciences depends upon 'subjective presuppositions,' which affect our judgments of what is significant and worth knowing. In a justly famous passage, he excluded the possibility of a stable system of concepts from which cultural reality can be deduced. Instead, he expected the viewpoints inspiring historical and social inquiry to be renewed again and again, unless an 'ossification' of intellectual life puts an end to inquiry itself.[20]

This brings us to the first crucial difference between Weber's and Rickert's methodologies of the historical and cultural sciences: for Rickert, the quest for 'objectivity' in these disciplines is tied to the more or less general validity of the cultural norms that shape judgments of value relatedness; for Weber, by contrast, such judgments are inevitably 'subjective.' According to Weber, 'objectivity' in the cultural and social sciences is therefore attainable only in the form of well-founded empirical observations and causal claims *about* some aspect of cultural reality, *not* in the 'subjective' concerns that initially favor particular lines of inquiry.

> It certainly does not follow (from the 'subjectivity' of the values inspiring scholarship) that research in the cultural disciplines can only have results that are 'subjective' in the sense that they are valid for some and not for others. What changes, rather, is the degree to which they *interest* some and not others.

The point is central for Weber; he made it again and again, and yet it is all too often evaded or misunderstood. Here, for emphasis, is what he wrote about singular causal claims.

> [The causal] attribution is undertaken, in principle, with the aim of being an 'objectively' valid truth of experience . . . and

20. Weber, "Objektivität," pp. 175–184, esp. p. 180; "Studien," pp. 251–256.

only the adequacy of the evidence determines . . . whether that aim is actually reached. . . . What is 'subjective' in a certain . . . sense is not the determination of the historical 'causes' for a given 'object' of explanation, but the delimitation of the historical 'object' . . . itself; for that is decided in terms of value relations, the 'conception' of which is subject to historical change.

These passages surely demonstrate that Weber considered it possible to reach objectively valid claims in the cultural and social sciences, despite the subjectivity involved in the selection and delimitation of their objects of study. Of course one can ask whether Weber was right or wrong in this opinion, and we will return to that question. In the meantime, there can be no doubt about the radical divergence between Rickert's and Weber's positions on at least one decisive problem of method.[21]

As a matter of fact, there were other, equally important differences as well. First, Rickert developed no fully coherent account of singular causal relationships, although he echoed Simmel and put forward a number of undeveloped suggestions on the subject. Weber, by contrast, offered a distinctive model of singular causal explanation that drew upon the work of the physiologist and statistician Johannes von Kries and upon a whole tradition in German legal theory. Stephen Turner and Regis Factor have most recently commented upon Weber's concepts of 'objective possibility' and 'adequate causation,' which freed him from the widely accepted equation of causal explanation with deduction from deterministic laws.[22]

Second, Rickert had almost nothing to say about the interpretation of actions and beliefs, and what he did say simply perpetuated the primitive view of 'understanding' as an empathetic identification or 'reexperiencing.' Here Weber was probably inspired by Simmel, rather than by Rickert. In any case, he developed a sophisticated and still compelling model of interpretation.

21. Weber, "Objektivität," pp. 183–184, including for first quote; "Studien," pp. 261–262, esp. p. 261.

22. Turner and Factor, *Weber*, esp. pp. 119–135.

Third, one cannot imagine Weber's methodological stance apart from his doctrine of 'ideal types,' which had no antecedent in Rickert's philosophy. As Friedrich Tenbruck has argued, this vital element in Weber's conceptual apparatus almost certainly owed more to the work of Carl Menger than to any other source.[23]

Fourth, Weber was a consistent and passionate champion of 'ethical neutrality' in scholarship and university teaching. Wilhelm Hennis has rightly urged us not to consider Weber's preoccupation with this issue a purely theoretical one. It grew partly out of his political and personal involvement in the controversies within the Social Policy Association. It also reflected his critical attitude toward aspects of the German university system, and his deepest commitments as an educator.[24] What is most noteworthy about Weber as a methodologist, however, is his determination to reconcile 'subjectivity' in the delimitation of research problems with 'objectivity' in the results obtained.

It is hard to understand and impossible to accept the view that Weber was essentially a follower of Rickert, a view proposed by Thomas Burger and fully developed by Guy Oakes. Oakes is particularly puzzling on the subject, since he concedes that Rickert's formulations were often imprecise or flawed. Nevertheless, he seems to conclude that Weber can be blamed for failing to resolve problems in Rickert's philosophy that were presumably inescapable, and not just misconceived.[25] My own view is closer to those of Dieter Henrich, H. H. Bruun, and W. G. Runciman. In his still classic analysis of Weber's methodology, Henrich emphasizes Weber's lack of interest in epistemological issues, his commonsense realism about the past, and his indifference to Rickert's obsession with the possibility of transcendentally valid cultural norms. Runciman suggests that Weber overstated his debt to Rickert, while understating his obligation to other precursors, particularly Simmel. Runciman also believes that Weber still made too much of the issue of value relevance in the historical and cultural sciences. He observes that all

23. Tenbruck, "Genesis der Methodologie."
24. Hennis, "Volle Nüchternheit."
25. Burger, *Max Weber's Theory;* Oakes, *Weber and Rickert.*

systematic knowledge depends upon *some* presuppositions, including the assumption that knowledge is worth having. Moreover,
natural scientists too sometimes deal with singular phenomena—and choose their objects of study in partly or wholly arbitrary
ways.[26] But while this criticism of Weber may be partly justified, the
problem of defining what is to be described and explained is surely
substantially more serious in the cultural than in the natural sciences.

Weber and Rickert also differed in their overall attitudes toward
the issues raised during the crisis of German academic culture.
Rickert single-mindedly opposed 'positivism' and championed the
new 'idealism.' He was not only preoccupied with the irrelevance of
'mass phenomena' and the importance of 'great men' in history; he
also developed holistic accounts of historical developments and
social groups as unique constellations of unique particulars, if not as
'essences.' But Weber consistently repudiated such notions. More
generally, Weber's reaction to the controversies of his day was not
as one-sided as that of Rickert—and certainly more complex than
some commentators have recognized.

Against Naturalism, Holism, and Irrationalism

One way to approach Weber's methodological orientation is to ask
what viewpoints he *opposed*. Many of his relevant writings, after all,
were critical essays. It seems only natural to ask what positions he
most consistently repudiated. And in fact, his critical targets easily
fall under the three main headings of 'naturalism,' organic holism
or essentialism, and 'irrationalism.' Under the heading of 'naturalism,' Weber opposed doctrines that most of his contemporaries
called 'positivist.' Following Rickert in this respect, he traced the
root of various naturalistic fallacies to the belief that the search for
universal laws is the only legitimate aim of knowledge, and that the
cognitively significant is therefore identical with the recurrent and
the lawful. Despite the resistance of German philosophical Idealism
and of the German historical schools, Weber wrote, the dramatic

---

26. Henrich, *Einheit der Wissenschaftslehre;* Bruun, *Science, Values, and Politics,*
esp. pp. 95–120; Runciman, *Critique.*

success of the natural sciences in the century of Darwin fostered a dogmatic commitment to the single cognitive strategy of abstracting from reality what can be subsumed under predictive generalizations. This cognitive commitment further suggests both that the singular as such is not worth knowing, and that reality may be fully deduced from universal laws. The typical naturalist assumes, more or less consciously, that the state of the world at any time can be known in its infinite complexity—and apart from the equally endless complexity of the preceding state.[27]

Also under the heading of 'naturalism,' Weber attacked a form of reductionism he (conventionally if unfairly) traced to Comte's notion of a 'hierarchy of sciences.' This was the thesis that the more 'general' disciplines near the bottom of the cognitive 'hierarchy' always provide the theoretical foundations for the 'higher,' more complex disciplines, a thesis that again implies a single cognitive aim, as well as the deducibility of particular realities from general laws. Weber's most explicit repudiation of this view was more specifically a critique of the chemist Wilhelm Ostwald, a member of the scientistic Leipzig Circle that also included the psychologist Wilhelm Wundt and the historian Karl Lamprecht. Ostwald provided Weber with an ancillary account of 'naturalism' as a dilettante's attempt to raise the insights of his particular discipline, most often a natural science, to the status of a *Weltanschauung,* a partly evaluative overall view of the world. The various forms of Social Darwinism were perfect examples of this syndrome.[28]

In the case of Ostwald's 'energetic' theory, the relevant thesis made it the twofold aim of culture (1) to maximize the availability of 'raw energy,' and (2) to optimize the conversion of 'raw' into 'usable' energy. On the basis of this stipulation, Ostwald was able not only to discern 'progress' in history, but also to recommend such strategies as the minimization of social conflict through legal regulation. To all this, Weber reacted in scathingly critical terms, not only as a methodologist, but also as a pedagogue and a critic of

27. Weber, "Objektivität," pp. 172–174, 186–188.
28. Weber, "Energetik," pp. 400–401, 406–407, 411–413, 422–423, 425–426, including for the following paragraph.

contemporary culture. He observed that the most 'energetically' efficient machine was the unaided human body—and that artistic activity was clearly 'wasteful.' Fairly or not, he portrayed submission to the existing power relations as maximally 'efficient' in Ostwald's scheme; freedom of thought was surely inconsistent with the technological utilitarianism of 'energetic' theory. Finally, Weber strenuously objected to Ostwald's exclusively instrumental view of knowledge as a means of manipulating the environment.

Prominent among the naturalistic reductions that Weber sought to discredit was the doctrine that interpretations of human actions and beliefs can be deduced from the laws of psychology. He did not mean to exclude the possibility that psychologists or biologists might some day clarify the relationship between the mental and the physiological; in the meantime, he regarded the two as conceptually separate realms. Like all other disciplines, he thought, the cultural sciences are grounded in ordinary experience, not in psychophysical axioms. Historians and social scientists develop and refine their terms and methods in the light of their own cognitive strategies. They must often draw upon the knowledge accumulated in other fields, including psychophysics, psychiatry, and the whole spectrum of the natural sciences. Nevertheless, their relationship to these other disciplines is by no means simply deductive.[29]

A more specific target of Weber's attack upon 'psychologism' was the view held by several prominent historical economists, including Schmoller and Lujo Brentano, that the Austrian theory of marginal utility was an application of a psychophysical law. Brentano explicitly claimed that the declining utility of added increments of a good could be deduced from the so-called Weber-Fechner law, also known as the 'basic' law of psychophysics. According to that law, added increments of a physical stimulus call forth decreasing sensory responses or discriminations. (The difference between weights of 51 and 52 pounds is harder to 'feel' than that between weights of 1 and 2 pounds.) Weber could find no more than a vague analogy between this psychophysical finding and the marginalist model in neoclassical economics. He pointed out that the personal 'needs' weighed by the

29. Weber, "Objektivität," pp. 173, 188–189; "Knies," p. 57.

economic agent of marginalist theory are not simply physiological, and that the weighing takes place in the context of scarce means and 'market' competition. The economic agent is engaged in purposive rational action, not in reflex reactions to physical stimuli. Like Menger, Weber saw economic theory as a hypothetical construct rather than an empirical generalization; it predicts how the 'ideal' economic man will act under certain specified circumstances, not how individual or even average human beings can be expected to behave in complex situations. The analytical tactics pursued by the theoretical economist thus differ radically from those of the German psychophysical tradition.[30]

In a further example of 'psychologism,' Wilhelm Wundt himself advanced a thesis that vaguely resembled Ostwald's 'energetic' speculations. Wundt argued that in certain causal relationships, the effects are somehow 'contained' in the causes. In certain culturally relevant psychological processes, however, 'creative syntheses' convert ordinary antecedents into dramatically new and culturally 'higher' or more significant phenomena. Needless to say, Weber was not impressed with this all-too-convenient thesis, or with Wundt's even broader 'law' about the long-term 'growth of psychic energy.' While objecting to the confounding of causal claims with value judgments, he pointed out that the formation of a diamond is no less or more 'creative' than the transformation of a prophet's intuitions into a new religion. He grouped Wundt's 'psychologism' with naturalistic meta-theories based upon mechanics or biology. What he particularly disliked about such expansions of disciplinary insights into *Weltanschauungen* was the false aura of scientific exactitude that clearly enhanced their popularity. Altogether, Weber had little respect for the Leipzig Circle, which of course included Lamprecht along with Wundt and Ostwald. In some of his letters, as well as in published footnotes and asides, he expressed contempt for Lamprecht's "psychologizing conceptual dialectics" and his vision of history as applied social psychology. One finds it hard to decide what irritated him more about

30. Weber, "Grenznutzlehre," pp. 384–397; see also *MWG* II/5, pp. 333, 578–579.

Ostwald, Wundt, and Lamprecht: their scientistic pretensions or their hopeless dilettantism.[31]

Some scholars see Weber strictly as an opponent of naturalism or 'positivism'; but this is a one-sided view. In fact he also questioned major assumptions of the German historical tradition and of the historical school of economics. Along with naturalism, he distrusted every form of methodological holism, organicism, or essentialism, all of which were problematic outgrowths of the principle of individuality. His position on these subjects emerges clearly enough in his commentaries upon Wilhelm Roscher and Karl Knies, two founding fathers of the older historical school of economics. Both Roscher and Knies treated peoples or nations as organic totalities, rather than as organized groups of individuals. Hypostatizing the 'soul' of a people, they were able to make it the 'cause' of the sociohistorical patterns they actually observed. In trying to avoid the isolation of economic practices from the rest of a nation's culture, they ended by assigning a peculiar guiding force to the 'spirit' of the people. That spirit became a metaphysical entity, an essence that could serve as the source of its expressions or 'realizations.' Weber saw traces of Hegelian thought in this line of argument, which he called 'emanationism' *(Emanatis-mus)*. My own sense is that it was a surrogate for more 'mechanical' models of change, which were excluded by the principle of individuality. I also believe that the word 'essentialism' will do in place of 'emanationism.' In the case of Roscher, the syndrome became oddly linked with the search for 'laws' of historical development. As Weber noted, the pertinent generalizations had to be about the 'class' of nations discussed by economic historians; indeed, they had to deal with parallels in the 'life cycles' of these 'individualities,' about stages in their evolution and eventual decline. Fortunately, as Weber also observed, Roscher's commitment to this form of 'historical economics' did not prevent him from drawing upon classical theory in his accounts of particular phenomena.[32]

31. Weber, "Knies," pp. 49–63; *MWG* II/5, p. 25, for quote on Lamprecht; "Roscher," pp. 7–8, 23–24, and "Knies," pp. 56, 63, for notes and asides on Lamprecht.

32. Weber, "Roscher," pp. 9–24; "Knies," pp. 142–144.

Weber's persistent methodological individualism was not, as far as we know, a reaction to the social holism of his French colleague Emile Durkheim, but mainly a safeguard against the holistic aberrations of the German historical tradition. In the same way, his strenuous causalism and his insistence upon the rationality model of interpretation cannot be understood apart from his comments upon what he called the 'problem of irrationality.' Weber himself occasionally characterized the concrete reality of immediate experience as 'irrational,' in that it is not fully encompassed even in our descriptions of singular objects and events. When he wrote about the 'problem of irrationality' in the work of Knies and others, however, he was referring to an altogether different issue. He noted that many historians and historical economists habitually divided reality into two distinct realms. One of these was the world of 'necessity' and causal determination, of natural forces and collective 'conditions'; the other was the realm of 'accident' and especially of 'free' human action. The use of this binary scheme was a reaction to the view that causality implies lawfulness and determinism, a view held not only by such targets of Weber's criticisms as Roscher and Knies, Eduard Meyer, and Rudolf Stammler but also by the hugely influential Schmoller. Apparently, it was the specter of determinism that drove many historians into a speculative defense of 'free will' that struck Weber as methodologically disastrous. Such prominent historians as Heinrich von Treitschke and Friedrich Meinecke considered it the dignity of human beings that their actions were 'free' in the sense of being *incalculable*. This made history inexplicable in principle, and of course it encouraged an emphasis upon the deeds of 'great men,' as against the determined and determining role of structural 'conditions.' So anxious was Weber to expose this fallacy that he turned an obligatory retrospective on the work of his academic predecessor Knies into a 'pretext' for an attack upon the syndrome, only to come back to it in his essays on Meyer and on Stammler.[33]

Weber dealt with the 'problem of irrationality' in several ways. If 'freedom' means incalculability, he wrote at one point, we will find

33. Weber, "Roscher," pp. 34–37; "Knies," pp. 44–46, 137; "Studien," pp. 218–219; "Stammler," p. 364.

no more of it in the interactions of human beings than in the evolution of local weather conditions. (A similar point had earlier been made by John Stuart Mill.) More important, as Weber tried to make clear, both 'determinism' and 'free will' are meta-scientific, transcendent speculations that have no relationship at all to the analytical practices of the cultural and historical sciences. Schmoller's occasional remarks upon the 'subjection of man' to the 'causal nexus' struck Weber as extra-scientific—and highly problematic—professions of faith. For the work of the cultural and social sciences, Weber continued, 'necessity' in the sense of full explicability is an infinitely distant goal, a cognitive ideal, but also an indispensable *maxim* in Kant's sense of that term. Conversely, the 'freedom' or incalculability of individual actions as a guide to the historians' practice is simply meaningless; for historians *do seek to explain* such actions. The choice among a plurality of possible actions, considered as an object of empirical investigation, is quite as 'determined' in principle as any particular event in nature. This is not to say, of course, that there is a single law, or even a finite set of laws, that could 'determine' all future actions. But then full reality cannot be deduced from laws in any case.[34]

Both Eduard Meyer and Rudolf Stammler tried to rescue the 'freedom' of actions by distinguishing between a prospective and a retrospective view of them. In retrospect, they argued, what has been done seems 'necessary,' or at least explicable in principle. Courses of action still in progress, however, seem open to alternate possibilities; the choices being made are not inevitable. Stammler added that without the awareness of multiple options, the agent's sense of *choosing* would be an illusion, which is hard to believe. In response to these considerations, Weber pointed out that in 'dead' nature too, particular series of events are more fully describable in retrospect than in prospect. To predict a specific outcome in detail requires vast knowledge of the anterior conditions and causal relations involved. (Knowing that a section has just broken off an overhanging cliff, we cannot say how the moving mass of stone will eventually be broken up and distributed.) We simply know more

34. Weber, "Knies," pp. 63–65, 136–137; "Stammler," pp. 366–368.

about a complex set of processes after than before they have occurred. As for the agent's sense of choice, it is certainly not an
illusion, and there is no need to deny its causal significance. What
would be illusory is an insistence upon the causelessness of actions
on the basis of an "indeterminist metaphysics." The claim that 'free
action' is causally relevant can only mean that the agent's 'resolve'
to act in a certain way is *both understandable and productive of
consequences.* Even a rigorous determinist, Weber thought, would
not object to that. The whole debate about 'free will' and 'determinism' in history is thus radically misconceived—and irrelevant to
empirical inquiry in any case.[35]

Finally, Weber argued that individual actions are less 'irrational'
in some ways than particular events in inanimate nature, for human
actions may be interpretable as *rational* ones. The relevance to the
issue of 'freedom' and 'determinism' is clear: as Weber pointed out,
it is precisely 'free' actions that are least 'irrational' in the sense
required by the champions of indeterminism. 'Free' agents are
characteristically unconstrained by physical and psychological forces
beyond their control. They can pursue deliberate ends through
means rationally selected to achieve them. And the 'freer' they are
in this respect, the more 'calculable' their actions are. No one is
more predictable than the principled and rational agent. The romantic counterimage of *gratuitous* deeds actually violates our sense of
what it means to act in conscious freedom; it puts us on a level with
animals. Our subjective sense of freedom *requires* that we be aware
of our ultimate commitments, as well as of our intermediate objectives, and that we exclude all but rational considerations in making
our moves. Of course most human actions are not fully rational in
this sense. Yet the specific incalculability suggested by the romantic
view of 'freedom,' Weber wrote, is the "privilege of—the madman."
'Freedom' and 'explainability' just aren't opposed to each other in
the way some historians think they are.[36]

It should now be clear that Weber was not an uncritical heir of
the German historical tradition. On the one hand, he challenged

35. Weber, "Studien," pp. 221–222; "Stammler," pp. 364–367.
36. Weber, "Knies," pp. 67, 132–133; "Studien," pp. 226–227.

certain forms of naturalism, and he persistently stressed the legitimacy of our interest in historical knowledge about *particular, culturally significant* objects, persons and events. On the other hand, he also sharply questioned a whole series of loose metaphors and methodological aberrations associated with the principle of individuality, including organic holism, the essentialist tactic, and the recourse to 'irrationality' as an escape from 'necessity.' Weber's true project, in other words, was to revitalize and extend the German historical tradition, not merely to perpetuate it. He meant to make it applicable to a new and wider set of sociocultural questions, to lay the foundations for a more systematic historical study of modern society. But he could not hope to reach his goal without first purging his scholarly heritage of some of its more problematic accretions. To me, his stance was typical of the 'modernist mandarin,' and I say this primarily in response to two distinguished German commentators upon Weber, who defend a more one-sided view.

Thus Wilhelm Hennis portrays Weber as a passionate opponent of 'Western' classical economics and of the 'Western' doctrine of 'natural rights.' According to Hennis, Weber was also an almost excessively imitative student of Knies's substantive work in economic history. Yet Weber distorted his teacher's theoretical reflections in a way that borders on the 'ignoble'; for he converted what should have been a customary appreciation of his academic predecessor into an occasion for a largely irrelevant methodological polemic. After all, Weber admitted that his essay on Knies was a 'pretext' for a discussion of the 'irrationality' issue. Hennis might be right if he could demonstrate that the notion of 'irrationality' did not play a distorting role in Knies's theorizing, or that it is essentially trivial. But he has almost nothing to say on these subjects.[37]

In an essay that is already quite old, Friedrich Tenbruck characterizes Weber's intellectual field much as some of Weber's contemporaries would have characterized it. The "sterility of positivism," he argues, was a serious threat to the German historical tradition of

---

37. Hennis, "Wissenschaft vom Menschen." Wilhelm Hennis is an insightful commentator on Weber in other important respects.

the later nineteenth century. Fortunately, it gave place to the intellectual revitalization of a specifically German form of history that was "idealist and intuitionist" in orientation. Thus when Lamprecht engaged in his misguided experiments, the German historical profession rose against him "in complete unanimity" *(wie ein Mann)*. Against this background, Tenbruck describes Weber's essays on Roscher and Knies as documents of "helplessness and sterility." Fortunately, Weber was generally a single-minded champion of the German historical tradition against the errors of 'positivism' and 'naturalism.' Tenbruck's only further qualification has to do with Weber's own occasional 'positivist' inclinations, which produced the "curious spectacle of a passionate attack upon naturalism on the basis of naturalist positions." Tenbruck defines neither 'positivism' nor 'naturalism,' and he names only Lamprecht as a representative of either. But then he cannot explain how 'positivism' could have been a major force in German scholarship even while the German historical profession unanimously condemned Lamprecht. These flaws and contradictions in Tenbruck's account would be 'curious' indeed, if they were not linked to his defense of the German historical tradition against the heretical view that by about 1900, it was methodologically and politically reactionary.[38]

Against Hennis and Tenbruck, I would side with Thomas Burger, who has provided a thoughtful analysis of the German historical tradition, particularly of Gustav Droysen and Heinrich von Treitschke. Burger recognizes that Weber was dissatisfied not only with the vision of a nomological history but with aspects of the dominant historiography as well. This further allows Burger to see the continuity underlying Weber's long-term shift of emphasis from a predominantly historical to a more explicitly sociological terminology. Burger rightly suggests that Weber ultimately revived Robert von Mohl's project for a systematic study of society, which had been repudiated by the German historical profession. Weber's position was consistent, according to Burger, because he shared some of

38. Tenbruck, "Genesis der Methodologie" (1959), esp. pp. 577, 583, 593–598. See also Tenbruck, "Weber und Meyer," in which Tenbruck tries to do for Meyer what Hennis tries to do for Knies, while also defending the German historical tradition as a whole against its unnamed but wrongheaded critics.

Mohl's objectives even when his language was mainly historical, and he did not abandon his interest in the historically singular even when he wrote more explicitly as a sociologist. Interestingly enough, Burger's position is consistent with the tenor of a recent essay by Tenbruck. Without altogether abandoning his former perspective, Tenbruck now sees Weber's methodology as a coherent and central element in his thought. Weber certainly repudiated Lamprecht's scientistic ambitions, insisted upon the cognitive interest of the singular, and emphasized the need for judgments of value related-ness. But as Tenbruck now acknowledges, Weber also broadened the German historical tradition in the light of changing economic and social conditions. The inherited practices of historical analysis had to be adapted to deal with new kinds of aggregate data, and to address social and structural issues it had formerly ignored.[39] This view I am able to share; but I really prefer a fuller and more specific characterization. Weber was neither an opponent nor a passive heir of the German historical tradition; he was neither a positivist nor an idealist. He was a *causalist* in a sense that I will now try to specify.

39. Burger, "Deutsche Geschichtstheorie," esp. pp. 29, 44–66, 74–95; Tenbruck, "Wissenschaftslehre."

3

What set Weber apart from all other participants in the debate over the future of the historical, cultural, and social sciences in Germany around the turn of the century was his commitment to singular causal analysis. There is much to be said about this commitment—and about its impact upon other aspects of Weber's methodological position. Before these matters can be usefully discussed, however, one needs to work through the technicalities of a doctrine that Weber took over, with little modification, from the physiologist and statistician Johannes von Kries, who in turn built upon an established tradition in German legal philosophy. The considerations offered by von Kries, while couched in complex statistical terminology, were really just aids to the understanding of certain purely qualitative judgments. Nonetheless, we must begin by following von Kries's quasi-statistical arguments in some detail.

Objective Probability and Adequate Causation

The problem von Kries addressed was that of assigning responsibility in civil law cases, in which there is no question of criminal intent. To do this, one has to attribute effects to causes in particular circumstances, and thus to engage in singular causal analysis. Unlike Weber, von Kries categorically asserted that any state of the world is fully determined by the totality of its antecedents. Like Weber, however, he saw that reality cannot be fully described. Our statements of prior conditions are thus typically incomplete and conceptually general-ized, as are our descriptions of consequences. Given the gaps in our knowledge, we can only hope to estimate the likelihood of certain results in the light of stated antecedents. Before throwing a die, to be sure, we can specify the chance of a given result with mathematical precision; but the probability involved is low, and the outcome thus 'accidental.' In other cases of interest to lawyers and social scientists, however, we may be able to judge that a certain broadly described event is 'objectively probable,' given a generally stated antecedent, in that the range of possibly relevant additional conditions (known or unknown) *under which it will occur* is greater than the sum of further conditions under which it will *not* occur. Von Kries pointed out that claims about such matters must be based upon 'nomological knowl-edge' about links between events *of a certain type,* rather than on insight into concrete objects or unique relationships. For the rest, he clearly recognized the hypothetical character of his quasi-statistical remarks about the 'ratio' between factors favoring and inhibiting an outcome. His real purpose, in any case, was to develop a plausible, if essentially qualitative, account of singular causal reasoning.[1]

According to von Kries, we have nomological knowledge not only of invariant causal laws but also of probable causal connections, and it is this probabilistic knowledge we draw upon when we ask, in retro-spect, to what extent various causal factors or 'moments' contributed to a particular result. To inquire into the importance of a specific antecedent, we imagine it (counterfactually) absent or altered. In assessing the role of negligence in an accident, for example, we 'compare' the sequence of events that actually occurred with what could have been expected if 'normal' caution had prevailed. We may consider a factor causally relevant to an effect if the effect would not have occurred without it. Our probabilistic knowledge allows us to estimate the course of events *in the absence* of that factor; but we also seek to generalize upon the closeness of the relationship between 'the cause' and the *actual outcome.* Consider a carriage driver who gets

1. Von Kries, "Ueber den Begriff," esp. pp. 180–195. Von Kries wrote of objec-tive 'possibility' *(Möglichkeit),* rather than 'probability' *(Wahrscheinlichkeit),* since the latter term seemed to imply a degree of subjectivity; nevertheless, 'probability' is the best English term for what he meant.

drunk and loses his way. At some distance from his normal route, his passenger is struck by lightning. We do not hold the driver responsible for two related reasons: (1) his wandering from the regular route did not *increase the objective probability* of the passenger's being struck by lightning, and (2) we have no basis for a probabilistic generalization linking drunkenness in coachmen to their passengers' being harmed in thunderstorms. But suppose instead that the drunk driver's carriage turns over in a ditch: he is responsible because his drinking certainly increased the chance of the accident, and we are prepared to generalize upon the incident.[2]

Von Kries explicitly rejected a model of causation involving the *invariable succession* of two events or types of events, one of which is 'the cause,' the other 'the effect.' Although von Kries did not say so, this model can be traced to David Hume. It is typically associated with the idea of 'the cause' as a (physically, not logically) *sufficient* condition for the effect, which *invariably follows* upon the cause. Von Kries's objection to this conception was the practitioner's observation that events can rarely if ever be traced to single antecedents or causal factors. Nevertheless, we are often quite certain that a particular 'moment' within a complex of anterior conditions *increased the probability* of a given result, and that it would have done so even if some of the conditions had been partly or wholly altered. Von Kries further insisted that we ordinarily and rightly think of a causal factor as 'acting' or 'effecting' *(Wirken)* to *bring about* an outcome. These considerations led von Kries summarily to term an antecedent factor (A) the *'adequate cause'* of a given result (B), and (B) the 'adequate effect' of (A), if (A) 'favors' the occurrence of (B). Where a relevant antecedent does not thus favor an actual outcome, von Kries proposed to speak of 'accidental' causes and effects. The coachman's inebriation, for example, 'accidentally caused' his passenger to be struck by lightning.[3]

Von Kries clearly thought of a causally relevant antecedent as a (physically) *necessary* condition or cause, rather than a sufficient one. Both his 'adequate' and his 'accidental' causes *have to be* present for

2. Ibid., esp. pp. 195–201.
3. Ibid., esp. pp. 198, 201–203.

the result to occur, although they bring it about only in conjunction with various additional conditions. In the light of this conception, one can understand the most important of von Kries's remaining concerns and suggestions: he called attention to two particularly clear cases of adequate causation. First, we securely ascribe a *deviation* from a regularly recurring course of events (a train *not* passing safely through a junction) to an *alteration* in the normal antecedents (a switch *not* being properly set). Second, if a state of affairs has remained stable over a period of time, we confidently trace a *change* in it to the intrusion of a new causal factor. In both of these cases, moreover, the idea of causation as an 'active effecting' is reinforced; for a cause is seen to *change* a set of initial conditions, to *alter* a course of events, and thus to *bring about* a deviation in the outcome that could have been expected in its absence. The whole conception is dynamic; it deals in sequences and processes, rather than in successive but unconnected events. It also forced von Kries into the complexities of counterfactual reasoning. These have to do with the degree of generalization and abstraction necessary—and defensible—in the 'comparison' between imagined and actual antecedents, causal sequences, and outcomes. Even without following von Kries's reflections on these difficult issues, we may safely conclude that he recommended probabilistic generalizations primarily because he had to ground legal judgments about what would have happened if 'the cause' of a given outcome had been absent or altered.[4]

Max Weber was profoundly influenced by the work of von Kries, as well as by the related legal theories of his Heidelberg colleague Gustav Radbruch. After first mentioning von Kries's main concepts in his 1904 essay on "Objectivity," Weber fully and explicitly followed von Kries in the concluding section of Weber's 1906 critique of Eduard Meyer, which is subtitled "Objective Probability and Adequate Causation in Historical Analysis."[5] The context was pro-

4. Ibid., esp. pp. 203–205, 212–213, 218–220.
5. In addition to von Kries, see Radbruch, *Lehre*, pp. 333/9–337/13. Sophisticated recent discussions of 'objective probability' and 'adequate causation' as conceived by von Kries and especially by Weber are Wagner and Zipprian, "Methodologie," and Turner and Factor, *Max Weber*, esp. pp. 119–165. See also Turner and Factor's earlier "Objective Possibility."

vided by passages in Meyer's methodological and substantive works that seemed to call for clarification. Thus Meyer traced the outbreaks of the Second Punic War, the Seven Years' War, and the War of 1866 to the relevant decisions of Hannibal, Frederick the Great, and Bismarck. Other personalities might have chosen differently and thus changed the course of history, he claimed, but the question of whether these wars would have occurred in any case was unanswerable and therefore "idle." Yet Meyer elsewhere described the two untraced shots that provoked street battles in Berlin during March of 1848 as "historically irrelevant," since social and political conditions made some sort of upheaval inevitable in any case. In his history of antiquity, finally, Meyer portrayed the Battle of Marathon as a turning point in Western history, in that it ensured the survival of Hellenic culture in the face of a theocratic alternative that was a distinct possibility until the threat of Persian domination was turned aside.[6]

In response, Weber systematically examined the methodological foundations of singular causal claims.

> To begin with, we ask . . . how the attribution of a concrete 'result' to a single 'cause' is . . . feasible . . . in principle, given that in reality it is always an infinity of causal factors that brought about the single 'event,' and that strictly all of these . . . causal factors were indispensable for the achievement of the result.

Excluding the idea of reproducing the totality of concrete conditions jointly sufficient for an outcome, Weber outlined the analytical tactics proposed by von Kries. Somehow, a complex of antecedent conditions has to be conceptually isolated that more or less strongly 'favors' the result to be explained. The judgments of probability required for this purpose typically cannot be quantified; but one can

---

6. Weber, "Objektivität," p. 179; "Studien," pp. 266–290, esp. pp. 266–268, 273–274, and p. 288, note 1, where Weber describes himself as "plundering" the thought of von Kries. Following von Kries, Weber literally refers to objective "possibility" in German; but "probability" nevertheless seems the better translation. See also Turner and Factor, "Objective Possibility."

focus upon selected potential 'causes' and compare the ranges of additional conditions under which they would, and would not, have brought about the effect in question. Meyer's thesis about the historical significance of the Battle of Marathon, for example, ultimately depends upon the judgment that a changed outcome of the Persian Wars would have made theocracy 'objectively probable.' Judgments of objective probability could be considered uncertain or 'subjective,' because they require the historian to *imagine* alternate causal sequences and outcomes. But as Weber pointed out, one does not have to know *exactly* what would have followed upon a Persian victory at Marathon to conclude that the Hellenic tradition might well have been altered by theocratic influences.[7]

The two concepts of 'objective probability' and 'adequate causation' are closely linked—and actually interdefined—in Weber's usage. Thus where an actual result was brought about by a complex of antecedent conditions that made it 'objectively probable,' 'the cause' may be called 'adequate' in relation to 'the effect.' Where a causal factor contributed to a historically interesting aspect of an outcome without being 'adequate' in this sense, it may be considered its 'accidental cause.' Some of Meyer's claims can thus be restated as follows: (1) a Persian victory at the Battle of Marathon would have made an alternate development of Western culture objectively probable, though not inevitable, and (2) the Persian victory would have been the adequate cause of this alternate development. (3) The Revolution of 1848 in Berlin was the adequate effect of prevailing social and political conditions, and (4) the two untraced shots were not even 'accidental' causes, since the upheaval would have occurred without them.[8]

When Weber first mentioned the concepts of 'objective probability' and 'adequate causation' in his 1905–1906 critique of Karl Knies, he cited two characteristic examples, one of which he repeated in his 1906 response to Eduard Meyer. The first was of a boulder dislodged from a cliff by a storm, which falls, shatters upon impact below, and disperses rock fragments over a certain area.

7. Weber, "Studien," esp. pp. 271, 277, 282–285.
8. Ibid., esp. pp. 286–287.

Weber's point was that we could neither predict nor fully explain the resulting distribution of fragments. We would be satisfied if, after the event, the actual outcome did not patently contradict our nomological knowledge about the processes involved. We could safely identify the storm's dislodging the boulder as the cause of what followed, and we would seek further explanation only if, for example, the final location of a particular rock fragment seemed inconsistent with our expectations. Weber further observed that in our explanation of the actual outcome, as in many similar cases of causal attribution, no empirically grounded judgments of necessity would be involved. The postulate of universal 'determinism' would accordingly remain extra-empirical, a "pure a priori."

In a second example, Weber referred to the throw of a die which presumably causes a given result, but again in ways we cannot specify. We therefore regard the particular outcome as 'accidental,' although we can state the probability of its occurrence with mathematical precision. If, after many throws, we find that certain outcomes are markedly more frequent than others, as a matter of fact, we confidently trace this (quantifiable) *deviation* from the 'accidental' distribution to some physical abnormality in the die. Drawing upon analogous illustrations, Johannes von Kries too had noted how securely we attribute a *deviation* from an expected pattern of events to an *alteration* in the normal antecedents. Weber provided a quantitative example, but his real intention was to argue for a looser, typically *qualitative* application of probabilistic reasoning to human affairs. What we want to know about a historical outcome in retrospect is what 'causes' can be identified as having 'favored' it to a more or less significant degree.[9]

Weber relied extensively upon the idea of 'objective probability'; but he insisted even more strenuously upon the role of counterfactual reasoning in causal analysis. If history is to rise above the level of the chronicle, he wrote in his commentary upon Eduard Meyer, then the historian must be explicit about *possible* developments that did *not* occur. Meyer had claimed that a defeat of the Greeks at Marathon would have had far-reaching cultural consequences; yet he had elsewhere rejected 'idle' speculations about what would have

9. Weber, "Knies," pp. 65–70; "Studien," pp. 284–285 for both examples.

happened if leading generals or statesmen had not decided in favor of war on certain occasions. In response, Weber stressed the need for just the sort of conjectures that Meyer accepted in practice but rejected in theory. According to Weber, we cannot assess the causal significance of an allegedly crucial political decision—or of any other possible cause—without trying to imagine what would have ensued in its absence. After all, a potentially infinite number of causal 'moments' or antecedent conditions have to be present to produce any concrete outcome. To identify significant singular causal relationships at all, therefore, we must inquire into the degree to which a particular cause 'favored' a given effect. But this in turn requires us hypothetically to 'compare' the result that actually followed with alternate possibilities. Thus historians need not apologize for their recourse to the "seemingly anti-deterministic category" of the merely possible, more or less probable. They cannot avoid reasoning, counterfactually, about historical events that did not occur, in order to identify the significant causes of what did occur.[10]

Here is Weber's simplest statement about the role of counterfactuals in singular causal analysis.

> The judgment that if a single historical fact in a complex of historical conditions [had been] missing or altered this would have brought about [*bedingt*] a . . . divergent course of historical events [is crucial in] the determination of the 'historical significance' of that fact.

Obviously, 'historical significance' here means something like 'causal influence' as further defined by the notions of 'favoring' and of 'adequate causation.' There is no reference to the issue of 'cultural relevance,' or to the grounds of the historian's interest in what is to be explained. The 'weighing' of possible causes is somewhat more completely described as follows.

> The first—and crucial—[abstraction involved in causal analysis] is just this: that among the actual causal components of a course

10. Ibid., pp. 266, 274–275.

[of events: *Verlauf*], we think of one or several as altered in a certain direction, and we ask ourselves whether, under the changed conditions . . . the same—or what other—outcome was 'to be expected.'

The point of counterfactual reasoning, for Weber, is a conjectural sorting and ranking of *possible* causes. That sorting and ranking takes place in the context of partly counterfactual reflections upon possible *courses* of events, *paths* of historical development that were more or less probable in the light of the possible causes under consideration. Weber's formulations about these matters were notably *dynamic*, and we will come back to the implications of that preference.[11]

In the meantime, we must not neglect one final point that Weber made again and again in his discussion of adequate causation. This has to do with the inescapably "abstract" character of causal analysis. In Weber's view, causal 'moments' are not simply given in immediate experience; they are constructs. On the one hand, we analyze the given into 'components,' "isolating" possible causes from the vast complex of surrounding antecedent conditions. On the other hand, we have to describe such potential causes at a certain level of generality. Like Simmel before him, Weber dismissed the project of following causal relationships to the microscopic level of necessary connections among elementary constituents of reality. Thus free from the tacit identification of explanation with either *reduction* or *reproduction*, however, he urgently had to point up the role of *description* in the formulation of singular causal claims. One consequence was that he saw no *logical* difference between causal questions about such specific events as the Defenestration of Prague and causal questions about such broad but singular phenomena as the rise of Western capitalism. The other consequence was that he undercut the rhetoric of 'uniqueness' that sometimes accompanied the defense of 'idiographic' knowledge. To substantiate individual causal claims at all, as Weber pointed out, both 'causes' and 'effects' must be described at a level of abstraction that will permit them to

11. Ibid., pp. 268, 273 for the two quotations.

be related to "rules of experience" *(Erfahrungsregeln)*. In Weber's account of these rules, they resemble imperfect empirical generalizations; they are incompletely universal and less rigorously formulated than full-fledged scientific laws. Often expressed in the language of common sense, they are subject to modification by various 'outside' influences. Even so, Weber explicitly considered them forms of "nomological" knowledge. Weber's model of singular causal analysis thus really excluded the illusion of a *radically* 'idiographic' historiography.[12]

The Frameworks and Tactics of Causal Analysis

We are now in a position to place Weber's account of causal analysis into the broader framework of his methodology on the one hand, and to explore some of its practical implications on the other. In pursuing these objectives, we will follow—but also extend—the pioneering work of Alexander von Schelting as well as the more recent commentary of Johannes Weiss.[13] Our starting point is a passage in Weber's essay on "Objectivity in Social Science and Social Policy," which conveniently brings together the several elements of his overall program. Drawing upon the contrast between a 'science of reality' *(Wirklichkeitswissenschaft)* and a 'law-seeking science' *(Gesetzeswissenschaft)*, Weber called for a "social science" that is concerned with the realities of social life in their "distinctiveness," that seeks to comprehend the "interconnection and the cultural significance" of particular phenomena "in their present-day form," along with "the grounds of their having historically become thus and not otherwise." The formulation is not particularly elegant, but it does identify all of the constituents of his cognitive objective.[14]

Weber begins by focusing upon the singular phenomenon to be explained. This *explanandum* is selected for analysis because it is culturally significant—or seems significant to the investigator—in its

---

12. Ibid., pp. 275–277.
13. Schelting, *Webers Wissenschaftslehre,* esp. pp. 255–268, 312–343; Weiss, "Kausale Durchsichtigkeit."
14. Weber, "Objektivität," pp. 170–171, for this and what follows.

distinctive contemporary form. The passage here reflects Weber's enduring concern with the *description* of singular objects, descriptions that must point up both what is significant about them and how they may fall under the terms of empirical "rules." But the study of these objects is by no means merely descriptive, and the illusion of 'reproduction' is absolutely excluded. For the cognitive strategy is to locate the explanandum in its "interconnection" with other singular phenomena. Finally, Weber calls for the kind of causal analysis that will explain why the course of historical development ultimately produced the explanandum *rather than* some other outcome. The projected investigation is clearly expected to deal in 'objective probability' and 'adequate causation'; but the formulation also implies counterfactual reasoning and a dynamic vision of alternate paths of historical change.

In his critique of Eduard Meyer, Weber urged practicing historians not to confound the genesis with the *justification* of particular interpretations or explanations. He conceded that historians might depend upon their "tact" and "intuition" in their reconstructions of the past. They might "understand" historical agents by drawing directly upon their own experiences. In writing their narratives, moreover, they might seek to evoke the total character of real persons and situations, so as to give their readers a sense of "reexperiencing" a historical world. Weber did not repudiate these aspects of historical practice; but he pointed out that mathematicians and natural scientists too may be inspired by initially unsubstantiated intuitions. In any case, he insisted upon separating the psychological origins of historical insights, along with their literary representations, from the "logical structure of cognition" and the "validity" of causal claims about the past. He saw the reconstruction of what he called the "causal regression," not narrative evocation or literary representation, as the historian's main task.[15]

Elsewhere in his article on "Objectivity," Weber enlarged upon the role of "nomological" knowledge in singular causal explanation. The attribution of particular outcomes to definite causal antecedents, he wrote, is simply impossible without such knowledge. The

15. Weber, "Studien," pp. 277–279.

ways in which historians make use of their experience and schooled imagination may vary from case to case; but the validity of their causal claims is bound to depend upon the reliability and comprehensiveness of what they know about *recurrent* connections. To be sure, their recourse is not likely to be to the strict laws typical of the natural sciences, but to "adequate causal connections expressed in rules." These rules function more as "means" than as ends in the cognitive strategies of the cultural sciences. Often there may be no point in explicitly formulating the everyday knowledge of human behavior that more or less dependably warrants a singular explanation. While the laws of the natural sciences are typically both general and abstract, the historian's rules of adequate causation tend to be richer in qualitative content, but also correspondingly less general. Nevertheless, the cultural and historical disciplines are by no means uninterested in the use—and even in the attempt to establish—relatively reliable 'rules of adequate causation.'[16]

Though less rigorous than the laws of the natural sciences, these rules do have a degree of predictive power. Their fallibility is due primarily to the fact that their terms—and the parameters of their applicability—are imprecisely specified, so that they are subject to alteration by intervening processes that could not be foreseen or conceptually isolated in advance. Weber pointed out that even such 'lawful' processes as the development of a fetus may be modified in unanticipated ways. The main problem of historical explanation lies in the sheer number of possibly relevant considerations. This also helps to explain why the cultural and social sciences are so much more successful in their retrospective explanations than in their predictions; they simply need the additional information that becomes available about a course of events only after it has been completed. *After the fact,* too, the historian knows much more about a situation in the past than the agents who confronted it at the time.[17]

Referring back to the examples of the falling boulder and the thrown die, Weber pointed out that we are often satisfied if what

16. Weber, "Objektivität," pp. 178–180.
17. Weber, "Studien," pp. 228–230, 267.

actually happens does not *contradict* our nomological knowledge. Here again, singular causal analysis can only be called "indefinite." Excluding well-founded judgments of necessity, it leaves the postulate of universal determinism a "pure a priori." Even so, Weber clearly regarded the study of singular cultural and social phenomena as valuable not only because they interest us in their own right, but also because the admittedly tentative discriminations involved in singular causal analysis may pave the way for more reliable 'rules of adequate causation.' In his 1907 critique of Stammler, Weber distinguished between causal laws, on the one hand, and empirical generalizations that offer no insight into causal relationships, on the other. He then argued that the term 'science' *(Naturwissenschaft)* might in fact be broadly defined to encompass all disciplines committed to the "empirical-causal explanation" of reality. Whether or not this passage signals a slight shift of emphasis in Weber's thinking by 1907, it has moved us far away from the thought of Heinrich Rickert.[18]

Indeed, one begins to understand why some commentators consider Weber a 'positivist' after all; but again, he was more specifically and properly a *causalist.* Any remaining doubts on that score can be removed, at the cost of some repetition, by considering the analytical *tactics* implied in some of Weber's passages on causal analysis. Here, for example, is another defense of counterfactual reasoning.

> The weighing of the causal significance of a historical fact begins with the question: whether with its elimination from the complex of factors under consideration as causally relevant [*mitbedingend*], or with its alteration in a certain manner, the course of events could, according to general rules of experience, have taken a direction that somehow diverged in character [from the actual one] in aspects decisive for our interest.

The sentence again posits a dynamic model of alternate historical sequences or paths. The influence of the presumptive cause is such

---

18. Weber, "Knies," pp. 65–66, 115; "Stammler," pp. 322–323.

that its removal or change would have led to a *deviation* from the *course of events* that has actually been observed.[19]

The idea of the cause (or its absence or alteration) accounting for the *divergence* between two possible directions of development is also present in the example of the die, which after repeated throws does *not* lead to an even distribution among the possible results. Von Kries had considered it particularly easy to trace deviations from normal or expected patterns to changes in the usual antecedents. Weber further insisted upon the recourse to 'general rules of experience.' Yet the role of such rules in the above passage is *not* to link the presumptive cause to the actual effect, but to support the claim that the *absence of the cause* would have been followed by a *divergent* course of events. We need not infer that Weber was uninterested in rules that connect causes to effects; but at least in the formulation just cited, he drew upon 'nomological' knowledge *exclusively* to sustain a projection about events that *did not occur*. As in many typical cases (mysterious shots unleashing a popular uprising), the *force* of a singular causal claim about the actual outcome depends *primarily* upon the reliability of the counterfactual thesis that results would have been different if 'the cause' had not intervened.

A revealing passage in Weber's critique of Meyer demonstrates how deeply he was committed to a dynamic conception of causal analysis. He confessed to seeing nothing wrong with historians describing certain conditions as "pressing toward" some particular outcome, citing "developmental tendencies," "moving forces," and even "impeding" factors in the course of history. He merely urged that such expressions not be held to represent "real causal interconnections" at an 'elementary' level, but as tactically useful constructs in the practice of historical reasoning. In his 1905 article on Knies, Weber further argued that the notion of causation actually encompasses two separate components. One of these is the idea of the cause "acting" *(Wirken)* to *bring about* an effect; the sense of agency here ties the cause to the effect. The other element in causation is the idea of conformity to observable "rules" or laws. Where the sciences reach the abstract level of quantitative equations, according

19. Weber, "Studien," pp. 282–283.

to Weber, the idea of the cause as agency can in practice be dropped or bracketed. Conversely, the idea of lawfulness becomes less important as the focus shifts to the links among qualitative particulars. In history and in the cultural sciences, Weber suggested, *both* components of causality come into play. The predominant cognitive aim is to identify qualitative causal connections among singular elements of reality; but there is a simultaneous interest in the use—and the extension—of nomological knowledge.[20]

The idea of cause as agency, which Weber found in the work of von Kries, drew criticism from Theodor Kistiakowski, who accused von Kries of having been misled by John Stuart Mill. According to Kistiakowski, Mill had imagined a kind of balance between factors tending to favor and factors tending to prevent a particular outcome. Von Kries had accepted Mill's account of 'objective probability,' including his problematic imagery of 'favoring' and 'impeding' antecedents, and he had thus arrived at an excessively "anthropomorphic" view of cause as agency. In response, Weber conceded that Mill had indeed introduced the notion of 'objective probability,' but added that von Kries had successfully demonstrated the difference between Mill's account of causation and his own. More interestingly from our point of view, Weber rejected the charge of anthropomorphism, while nevertheless continuing to insist upon an "active" view of the "causal ties" that link "series of individual qualitative changes."[21]

What ultimately emerges from Weber's formulations, in fact, is an image of causal relationships—and of causal analysis—that deals in *courses* of events, in counterfactuals, and in *divergences* between alternate *paths and outcomes*. To illustrate Weber's vision, we might begin by positing a *hypothetical* sequence of events from an initial state (A) to an eventual result (B). We next focus upon certain distinctive elements (A') within the initial state (A) that can be isolated as causally significant with respect to an *actually observed* path of development

20. Ibid., p. 290; Weber, "Knies," pp. 134–136.

21. Weber, "Studien," pp. 269–270. See Ritschl, *Causalbetrachtung,* esp. pp. 43–89, for an anthropological speculation about the experiential roots of causal reasoning, in which the notion of "acting" *(Wirken)* is indeed interpreted in an anthropomorphic sense. Weber was aware of Ritschl's work.

from (A') to (B'); if these elements (A') were absent, then the sequence (A-B) would ensue. Alternately and more conveniently, we imagine a *shift* in the antecedent conditions from (A) to (A'). In Weber's thinking, the *effect* of this alteration is a *deviation* in the subsequent course of events *and* in its outcome, such that the path (A-B), the hypothetical sequence in the absence of the cause, is replaced by the observed path (A'-B'), and the ultimate effect is the substitution of the actual effect (B') for the hypothetical result (B) that would have occurred if the cause had not intervened.

Figure 1 is a graphic representation of the scheme.

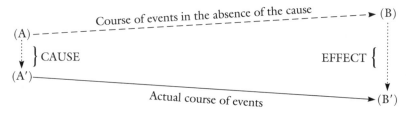

Figure 1

The dashed line (A-B) stands for a counterfactual claim about what would have happened if the cause had been absent or altered. The object of causal analysis is to explain the actual course of events from the region encompassing both (A) and (A') to the result (B'), *rather than to (B)*, by specifying the causally significant elements within (A) or the *difference* between (A) and (A'). In the terminology of von Kries and of Weber, that difference 'acts' to change the direction of historical development. The causal relationship is not just a repeated succession or 'constant conjunction' of two events. Instead, an *alteration* in a set of initial conditions 'makes a difference' by 'bringing about' an outcome that could not have been expected if the cause had not 'acted' as it did.

The claim that the shift from (A) to (A'), or the presence of (A') within (A), adequately caused the replacement of (B) by (B') rests upon the counterfactual argument that without the intervention of the cause, the objectively probable outcome would have been (B), rather than (B'). Explicitly or implicitly, historians who explain what actually happened must draw upon more or less formal 'rules of experience,' or upon other forms of 'nomological' knowledge. And they must do this not only to link (A') to (B'), but, often more urgently, to argue that the counterfactual sequence (A-B) was indeed to be expected in the absence of (A') within (A) or of the shift from (A) to (A'). That is the only way to show that (A') or the shift (A/A') really 'made a difference.' Von Kries and Weber both recognized that particularly convincing causal claims often trace *divergences* from expected courses of events to deviations in the normally prevailing initial conditions, as in the example of the train *not* successfully passing through a junction because the switches were not set, or in that of the frequently thrown die *failing* to yield an even distribution of results. Particularly in retrospect, to cite more typically historical examples, it is much easier to chart what actually followed upon the Battle of Marathon—or upon the untraced shots of 1848—than to defend counterfactual claims about the course of events in the absence of these possible causes. Nomological knowledge may thus be more often required to sustain counterfactual claims about hypothetical sequences than directly to link alleged causes to particular effects. Weber's model, to be sure, is complex indeed; but it is also richly suggestive. More important, I believe, it represents the historian's reasoning much more fully than simpler and less flexible schemes.

Notice that a counterfactual supposition about a certain course of events (A-B in Figure 1) can become the explanandum in a further stage of a complex causal analysis. In a statistical study of access to higher education, for instance, one might find oneself explaining a *short-term* acceleration in the rate of university entry against the *background* of *long-term* increases at a more moderate pace. Obviously, these long-term trends in turn demand explanation, which might depart from the counterfactual supposition of essentially *unchanging* rates of enrollment per age group. Practicing historians have probably always known, more or less tacitly, that long-term structural changes must be traced to long-term causes, while short-term phenomena must be linked to chronologically more specific antecedents. In any case, Figure 1 could easily be extended to encompass several stages of *long-term as well as short-term* causal argument, in each of which a deviation from a 'normal' or expected path of development is traced to an alteration in the initial conditions.

Notice, finally, that Weber's account of causal analysis is particularly hospitable to the interpretation and explanation of human actions. Thus if social scientists trace changes in rates of marriage to shifts in economic conditions, Weber argued, they seek "causal interpretations in terms of motives," trying to link alterations in the contexts of choice to changes in the courses of action pursued by typical agents. In the case of a decision made by Frederick the Great, to cite another of Weber's examples, a successful interpretation of his motives adds to our causal understanding. Weber left no doubt that the interpretive inquiry into motivations is a form of causal analysis in the same logical sense as any other search for 'adequate causes,' even though the causal connection between a motive and an action is never an instance of natural necessity.[22]

Contemporary Formulations

In David Hume's most typical formulation and in the usage of most philosophers today, a cause is a (physically) sufficient condition for the occurrence of the effect. To say that event (A) was the cause of event (B) is to claim that the occurrence of (B) could have been predicted from the occurrence of (A), and the empirical warrant for this claim is that events of type (A) have invariably been found conjoined with subsequent events of type (B). Carl G. Hempel, the most prominent contemporary heir of the Humean tradition, developed the so-called covering law model of explanation, in which to explain an event is to infer the statement that it occurred from (1) certain statements of initial conditions and (2) certain empirically established universal laws. The event-statement *(explanandum)* is inferred from the *explanans,* the statement of initial conditions and the law or laws that "cover" the case. In the "deductive nomological" variant of the covering law model, the explanandum event follows necessarily from the initial conditions and the nomological laws of the explanans. But Hempel also recognized a version of the

22. Weber, "Knies," pp. 68–70, 134.

covering law scheme in which the laws involved are of a statistical or probabilistic form, so that the explanandum event cannot be deduced with certainty from the explanans.[23]

Hempel further clarified his position in two respects. First, he indicated that a covering law explanation may be "incomplete": "elliptical," "partial," or a mere "explanation sketch." Second, he slightly qualified the thesis of "structural identity" or "symmetry" between explanation and prediction. While insisting that *in principle*, "a deductive-nomological explanation is potentially a deductive-nomological prediction," he acknowledged that retrospective explanation is easier than prediction in practice, simply because the explanandum event has actually occurred.[24]

Nevertheless, historians have found it difficult to accept Hempel's account of their practice. When they try to construct generalizations of which their causal explanations are presumably instances, they come up with 'laws' that are plainly vaguer and more doubtful than the singular claims they are supposed to sustain. ('When events resembling the assassination of Archduke Ferdinand occur under similar conditions, then events like the outbreak of the First World War invariably or usually follow.') Not surprisingly, historians can see no point in generalizations that are either vacuous or false. The suggestion that their explanations are mere sketches does not impress them, since they rightly judge their singular causal claims to be sounder than any parallel laws they might be taken to imply.

In any case, the Humean and Hempelian tradition has in recent years been qualified or questioned in a number of ways. Thus J. L. Mackie has identified a common use of the term 'cause' in which it is *not* a sufficient condition of the effect. What Mackie terms an 'INUS' condition is an *I*nsufficient but *N*on-redundant (Necessary)

---

23. Some of this and what follows is drawn from portions of Ringer, "Causal Analysis." For Hume's partly inconsistent formulations, see Mackie, *Cement of the Universe*, pp. 3–30. On the "covering law" model, see Hempel, "The Function of General Laws in History"; "Explanation in Science and in History"; "Reasons and Covering Laws in Historical Explanation."

24. Hempel, "Aspects of Scientific Explanation," pp. 415–425, 364–376. For a cogent defense of the symmetry thesis, see also Grünbaum, *Philosophical Problems*, pp. 281–313.

part of an *Un*necessary but *S*ufficient condition. By way of example, imagine someone smoking in bed and burning the house down. On the one hand, the smoker's carelessness was not sufficient *by itself* to start the fire, but it was certainly not causally irrelevant or redundant; nor, on the other hand, was it a necessary condition of the house burning down, since that disaster could have resulted from other accidents as well. Nevertheless, the fire set by the smoker was certainly sufficient, under the prevailing circumstances, to destroy the house. As a minimum, Mackie's clarification is a good deal more complex than the usual conception of the cause as a sufficient condition.[25]

The legal philosophers H. L. A. Hart and A. M. Honore have criticized the form in which John Stuart Mill passed along Hume's doctrine of constant conjunction, a doctrine in which a singular causal claim necessarily implies one or more universal laws, along with a complex set of antecedent conditions. Mill distinguished a 'philosophical' from a 'common' notion of causation: In strict philosophical terms, *all* of the relevant anterior conditions jointly constitute the (sufficient) cause of a particular effect, whereas our common usage singles out just one of these antecedents as 'the cause' of what we intend to explain. Commenting upon this aspect of Mill's analysis, Hart and Honore point out that commonsense causal claims do not seem to rest upon knowledge of invariant sequences, but upon looser generalities that may be downright platitudinous. (People you hurt usually won't like you afterward.) In the context of legal judgments about human actions, Hart and Honore really reject the identification of explanation with prediction. When the lawyer, the historian, and the common man claim that a person's action caused another person to behave in a certain way, for instance, they do not *mean* or *need* to assert that under similar circumstances, the same thing would happen again.[26]

According to Hart and Honore, moreover, there is no single concept of causation, but a group of concepts united by certain family resemblances. At the core of causal thinking, nevertheless,

25. Mackie, *Cement of the Universe*, p. 62.
26. Hart and Honore, *Causation in the Law*, pp. 8–23.

there lies the notion of human action that affects the environment, and that thus "makes a difference" in the "course of events." This sense of agency is central even where no human action is actually involved.

> The cause, though not a literal intervention, is a *difference* to the normal course which accounts for the difference in the outcome. . . . It is, moreover, a marked feature of these simple causal statements that we do not regard them as asserted . . . without warrant in a particular case if the maker of them cannot specify any considerable number of the further required conditions.

The first sentence here echoes Weber's sense of alternate paths, of the cause as a change in the initial conditions, of a deviation in the 'normal' course of events, and of the effect as an alteration in the outcome to be expected in the absence of the cause. The second sentence raises questions about Mill's idea of 'selecting' the 'cause' from among the relevant antecedent conditions. It is surely unrealistic to posit all of these conditions as fully known, whether in our common experience or in a typical scientific experiment. Thus if we add a few drops of an unknown chemical to salt water and there is a precipitation, we may safely conclude that the injection of the unknown reagent was the cause of the (unforeseen) reaction that took place. But the nomological knowledge that supports our conclusion may be no more than a sense that salt water tends to remain what it was unless something intervenes! Hart and Honore insist upon the huge *practical* difference between prediction and retrospective explanation. Elsewhere, they further point out that probabilistic generalizations cannot truly support singular causal explanations, for to argue that a given event was highly probable is not yet to know why it occurred in the case at hand.[27]

Partly inspired by Hart and Honore, Alasdair MacIntyre has pointed to a legitimate sense of the term 'cause' that is equivalent to "necessary, but not necessarily sufficient, condition":

27. Ibid., pp. 24–57, esp. pp. 27, 29.

For very often when we speak of 'the' cause of an event, for instance at a coroner's court in assigning responsibility for an accident, we point to a condition, by itself necessary but not sufficient for the occurrence of the accident. We do so when *events were in train* such that without the condition in question being satisfied the event would not have occurred. Taken by itself the condition was necessary but not sufficient. Taken in conjunction with all the other prior events, its satisfaction was sufficient to bring about the accident. So it is with the ice patch on the otherwise safe road.[28]

The claim about the ice patch is singular and retrospective. In the review of events at the coroner's court, it is known that there actually was an ice patch, and that an accident actually occurred. There is no suggestion that the accident could have been predicted, given all the prevailing conditions; for these conditions could not be fully spelled out. Of course the development of ice on a road surface increases the objective probability of accidents, as von Kries and Weber stressed. But no one believes in *invariant* laws linking ice patches to accidents. Attention at the coroner's court is focused, rather, upon the *train of events* in a particular case. The *dynamic* aspect of MacIntyre's model distinguishes it from Mackie's account of 'the cause' as an 'INUS condition.' The real question is whether the train of events would have led to the normal outcome of safe passage through the curve *if only* the ice patch had been absent. It is the *counterfactual* claim that the accident would not have occurred if the ice patch had not been present that identifies the ice patch as the cause of the accident. A great deal of reflection is nowadays devoted to the logical structure and the methodological problems of counterfactual argument. In certain experiments, one can 'control for' all but one of a set of initial conditions to test its causal efficacy, and the point of regression analysis is to assess how much of a given outcome may be ascribed to a particular element in a complex of possible causes. Even without pursuing the technical issues involved, we may conclude that Weber set many of the terms of present-day theories and practices.

28. MacIntyre, "Antecedents of Action," p. 196; italics mine.

The philosopher Donald Davidson, though generally perceived as continuing in Hempel's tradition, has sharply modified the received view of the relationship between singular causal explanation and the 'covering law' model in its deductive nomological form. Here are his decisive clarifications.

> We are usually far more certain of a singular causal connection than we are of any causal law governing the case. . . . Ignorance of competent predictive laws does not inhibit valid causal explanations, or few causal explanations could be made. . . . 'Windows are fragile, and fragile things tend to break when struck hard enough, other conditions being right' is not a predictive law in the rough—the predictive law, if we had it, would be quantitative and would use very different concepts. . . . *It is an error to think no explanation has been given until a law has been produced.* Linked with these errors is the idea that singular causal statements necessarily indicate, by the concepts they employ, the concepts that will occur in the entailed laws.[29]

These sentences do indeed remove the difficulties that arise if one assumes that singular causal explanations must be directly deducible from initial conditions and 'covering' laws; but they also reduce the relevance of the 'covering law' model for the practice of causal analysis. Suppose that historians have arrived at a genuine causal explanation, without any recourse to the 'covering law' theory. As clarified by Davidson, that theory now stipulates that their successful explanation *does* presuppose a law, though this law may not be known, and may not be couched in terms similar to those of the singular explanation. Isn't it reasonable to ask how the historians actually arrived at their causal claim—and why, no matter how they reasoned, their conclusion necessarily implies a law? Weber assigned an important explanatory function to nomological knowledge *broadly defined;* but I believe he would have remained agnostic with respect to the 'covering law model,' at least in its deductive no-

---

29. Davidson, "Actions, Reasons, and Causes," pp. 16–17; I have slightly changed the order of the sentences, and the italics are mine as well.

mological variant. Even when students of the cultural and social sciences explicitly cite or formulate lawlike generalizations, after all, the laws at issue are almost always inductive-statistical or probabilistic, rather than invariant and deterministic.

All the more important is the work Wesley Salmon has done on the 'statistical relevance model' of scientific explanation. In Hempel's analysis, statistical explanation figured as a variation upon deductive nomological explanation within the covering law scheme: with respect to a certain class of explanandum events, the statement that they occurred was deduced from the initial conditions and *statistical laws with a high probability*. But as Salmon points out, statistical causal explanation "involves a difference between two probabilities."

> What is crucial for statistical explanation . . . is not how probable the explanans renders the explanandum, but rather, whether the facts cited in the explanans *make a difference* to the probability of the explanandum. To test the efficacy of any sort of therapy . . . controlled experiments are required. By comparing the outcomes in an experimental group . . . with those of a control group . . . we procure evidence concerning the effectiveness of the treatment.
>
> In order to construct a satisfactory statistical explanation . . . we need a *prior probability* of the occurrence to be explained, as well as one or more *posterior probabilities*. A crucial feature of the explanation will be the comparison between the prior and posterior probabilities.

In the terminology we have been using, the prior probabilities report the outcome in the absence of the cause; the posterior probabilities report the outcome in the presence of the cause. The *divergence* between the two can be described as an alteration in the outcome that was *brought about* by the intervention of the cause.[30]

It should be noticed that Salmon, unlike Hempel, is committed to *causal* explanation. Thus he has challenged the received view of such noncausal generalizations as the ideal gas law.

30. Salmon, *Four Decades*, p. 59; Salmon, *Scientific Explanation*, pp. 33–34.

Non-causal regularities, instead of having explanatory force . . .
cry out to be explained. Mariners, long before Newton, were
fully aware of the correlation between the behavior of tides and
the position and phase of the moon. But inasmuch as they were
totally ignorant of the causal relations involved, they rightly
made no claim to any understanding of why the tides ebb and
flow. . . . Similarly . . . the ideal gas law had little or no explanatory power until its causal underpinnings were furnished by the
molecular-kinetic theory of gases. . . . We must give at least as
much attention to the (causal) explanations of regularities as we
do to explanations of particular facts. . . .

Developments in twentieth-century science should prepare us
for the eventuality that some of our scientific explanations will
have to be statistical—not merely because our knowledge is incomplete . . . but rather, because nature itself is inherently statistical. . . . By employing a statistical conception of causation . . . it
is possible to fit together harmoniously the causal and statistical
factors in explanatory contexts.

No longer a stepchild of deductive-nomological explanation, statistical analysis has here become the foundation of a new causalism.[31]

To illustrate his interrelated views of statistical and causal explanation, Salmon cites the incidence of leukemia among military
personnel who witnessed the testing of an atomic bomb in 1957 and
calls attention to several key features of this tragic case.

(1) The location of the individual at the time of the blast is
statistically relevant to the occurrence of leukemia; the probability of leukemia for a person located 2 kilometers from the
hypocenter of an atomic blast . . . is not high. . . . But it is
markedly higher than for a random member of the entire
human population. It is the *statistical relevance* of exposure to
an atomic blast, not a *high probability*, which has explanatory
force. . . .

(2) There is a *causal process* which connects the occurrence of

31. Salmon, "Why Ask, 'Why?'?," pp. 408–409.

the bomb blast with the physiological harm done to people at some distance from the explosion. . . .

(3) At each end of the causal process—i.e., the transmission of radiation from the bomb to the person—there is a *causal interaction*. . . . Each of these interactions may well be irreducibly statistical and indeterministic, but that is no reason to deny that they are causal.

Some probabilistic claims reflect deficiencies in our knowledge; but Salmon's main interest is in *irreducibly* statistical and indeterministic causal interactions.[32]

In the further development of his argument, Salmon defines and distinguishes (a) a process or *causal process* and a causal *interaction*.

In ordinary affairs a chance meeting with a friend in a supermarket would normally be considered an event; the entire shopping trip might qualify as a process. In microphysics a collision of a photon with an electron would constitute an event; an electron orbiting an atomic nucleus would qualify as a process. . . . Something that, in one context, would be considered a single process (such as running a mile) would often be considered a complex combination of many processes from another standpoint (e.g., that of a physiologist).

The collision of two billiard balls, and the emission or absorption of a photon, are standard examples of causal interactions. Interactions are the sort of things we are inclined to identify as events.

Clearly, Weber's strikingly dynamic view of singular causal analysis could be restated in terms of causal processes and causal interactions.[33]

At the ontological level, Salmon proposes to replace the vision of the world as a set of events—and of objects at particular locations in space and time—with reality as a network of causal processes and

32. Ibid., pp. 409–410.
33. Salmon, *Four Decades*, p. 108; "Why Ask, 'Why?'?," pp. 410–411.

interactions. This alternate view of reality, as Salmon suggests, also answers the questions initially asked by Hume about the connection between causes and effects.

> If we think of a cause as one event, and of an effect as a distinct event, then the connection between them is simply a spatio-temporally continuous causal process. This sort of answer did not occur to Hume. . . . [because he thought of] chains of events with discrete [causal] links, rather than processes analogous to continuous filaments.

Thus, as Salmon writes, "causal processes constitute precisely the causal connections that Hume sought, but was unable to find." Propagated across space and time, causal processes can interact, and that is how they bring about events.

> Causal processes *propagate* the structure of the physical world. . . . Causal interactions *produce* the structure and modifications of structure that we find in the patterns exhibited by the physical world.
> Causal processes transmit energy, information, structure, and causal influence; they also transmit propensities to enter into various kinds of interactions under appropriate circumstances.

A world characterized by the transmission of causal influences and propensities to interact, needless to say, is a more Weberian world than the world of constant conjunction and of deductive nomological explanation envisaged by Hume and Hempel.[34]
Salmon's network of processes is in some sense an open one, so that the structure of the world may be indeterministic.

> From the traditional standpoint, causality is incompatible with indeterminism—that is, to whatever extent . . . events are not completely determined, to that extent they cannot be explained

34. Salmon, "Why Ask, 'Why?'?," p. 411; *Scientific Explanation,* pp. 147, 132, 261.

causally. . . . [But] according to the explicitly probabilistic account of causality developed [here] . . . it is possible to provide *causal* explanations of ineluctably stochastic events.

Weber's agnosticism with respect to determinism, it seems, was even sounder than he knew.[35]

Nothing more vividly recalls Weber's account of singular causal analysis, finally, than Salmon's diagram of a *causal interaction*, in which two intersecting causal processes are both altered, and two new causal processes result. Figure 2 is an adaptation of Salmon's illustration.[36]

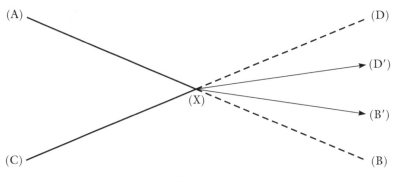

Figure 2

Suppose we focus upon one of the initial processes (A-X), and we conceive its interaction with the other process (C-X) as an intervening modification of (A-X). We can then regard the *deviation* of (X-B′) from the course (X-B)—along with the actual outcome (B′, *rather than* B), as an effect of the *modification* of the process (A-X) by the intervening (C-X). And what we arrive at strikingly resembles Weber's model of singular causal explanation, although it is certainly more complete.

Much of what contemporary philosophers have argued seems compelling. More important, the formulations I have cited can help us to appreciate Weber's occasionally difficult arguments. We begin to see why he refused to equate singular causal explanation with

35. Salmon, *Scientific Imagination*, p. 243.
36. Salmon, "Why Ask, 'Why?'?," p. 417.

deduction from predictive laws. We understand his interest in objective probability, and his essentially dynamic view of history as a network of alternate processes or developmental paths. We recognize the centrality of counterfactual and comparative analysis in the cultural and social sciences. We even begin to share Weber's agnosticism with respect to the issue of determinism. As we shall see in the next chapter, moreover, the tactic of interpreting Weber's texts in the light of convincing present-day formulations was strongly recommended by Weber himself.

INTERPRETATION AND EXPLANATION

4

Though firmly committed to causal analysis, Weber persistently emphasized the role of interpretation in the cultural and social sciences. He used the terms *Verstehen* (interpretive understanding) and *Deuten* (interpretation) to characterize this part of his methodological program; more rarely, he referred to *nachfühlend Verstehen* (empathetic understanding). At the same time, he always regarded interpretation as an element in causal analysis, writing of the need for 'interpretive explanation,' and ultimately recommending an 'interpretive sociology' *(verstehende Soziologie)*. This much is generally known; but we should look a little more carefully at the *way* in which Weber wedded interpretation to explanation.

From Interpretation to Causal Analysis

In his early (1904) essay on "Objectivity," Weber touched briefly upon the social scientist's effort "empathetically to understand" both "intellectual processes" and human behaviors, the latter on the basis of informal observation and "rules of rational action." He was anxious to challenge the view that the cultural, historical, and social sciences depend upon 'teleological' reasoning about human 'purposes' and intentions. To undermine this position, Weber redefined the *aim* of an action as its *cause*. For the cultural scientist, he wrote, a "'purpose' is . . . the image of an outcome that becomes the cause of an action." Agents envisage the results they hope to achieve, along with means of attaining these results, and that is what moves them to act. The specific characteristic of "this kind of cause," Weber added, is that we can "understand" it. From Weber's causalist perspective, in other words, the peculiarity of the cultural and social sciences has nothing to do with 'teleology'; but it does crucially depend upon accounts of actions that entail the "interpretive understanding" of their "causes." Weber never wavered from this early position; much of what he wrote after 1904 was intended to specify the methods of interpretation and the relationship between interpretation and explanation.[1]

In his 1905 critique of Karl Knies, for example, Weber drew a line between interpreting a written or spoken "expression" *(Äusserung)* on the one hand, and understanding the *motive* of an action on the other. In making this distinction, he explicitly followed Georg Simmel, with whom he nevertheless disagreed on subordinate issues. Simmel had argued that the 'objective' interpretation of what has been expressed and transmitted is based upon the 'logical' reconstruction of thought 'contents' that are 'objectively' available to the interpreter. (Some of our most reliable interpretations are of such written sentences as '2 + 2 = 4'). In thus focusing upon propositions (rather than spoken commands, for example), Simmel neglected the 'subjective' intentions of the speakers or writers whose 'expressions' were at issue. Dissatisfied with this limitation, Weber called for attention to the purposes of persons who made particular statements. But it was easiest for him to do this by enlarging upon the understanding of actions in terms of the agents' motives, which also struck Simmel as a separate problem.[2]

It was the 'motivational understanding' of actions or of action orientations that Weber chiefly had in mind when he stressed the explanatory significance of interpretation: "Any . . . science about human behavior . . . [including about] any intellectual act and any psychic habitus . . . seeks to understand this behavior, and thereby

1. Weber, "Objektivität," pp. 173, 183.
2. Weber, "Knies," pp. 92–95; see also "Grundbegriffe," p. 1. Much of Weber's discussion of interpretation was imbedded in a critique of the subjectivist psychology of Hugo Münsterberg; but his *positive* point of departure was the work of Simmel.

interpretively to explain its progression *[Ablauf]*." The difficulty of the passage stems from the fact that its main subject is an 'outward' *course of action,* but that in Weber's view, this 'progression' can be understood only in terms of 'inner' events and dispositions. Weber agreed with Simmel's observation that human behaviors are often very difficult to understand or to predict, since individuals may react to similar situations in dissimilar ways. But Weber pointed out that ordinary 'rules of adequate causation' typically fall short of full predictive power as well. He thus felt free to insist that the "interpretive investigation of motives" is a form of "causal attribution," and thus an integral part of the larger project of causal analysis in the cultural and social sciences. Consistent with this position, Weber held that the interpreter must try to determine what actually moved persons to act in particular cases. He warned against the view that the agents themselves are the most reliable informants about the grounds of their actions. Nor was he content to know what considerations *might reasonably* have motivated certain behaviors under specified conditions. It is the agent's *actual* motive that the investigator must seek to identify, since it was the true cause of the action that has to be explained.[3]

We must guard against two misreadings of Weber that are possible at this point. First, we should not attribute to him the identification of 'motives' with such broad dispositions as 'pride,' 'benevolence,' or 'greed.' Since he held that the cause of an action may be the agent's vision of an outcome, he was clearly referring to fairly specific aims, along with *beliefs about how to attain them.* Any doubts on that score are resolved by Weber's persistent emphasis upon 'purposively rational' *(zweckrational)* action as the most understandable type of behavior. As Weber noted in his essay on Knies, interpreters are well advised to begin by supposing that the actions they observe are rationally selected, usually to achieve specific ends. It is such purposively rational action that can create the false impression of 'teleology.' In reality, the image of a desired result is the *cause* of the action; but it can play that role only if it encompasses

3. Weber, "Wertfreiheit," p. 532 (for quote); "Knies," pp. 114–115, 134; "Studien," p. 282.

beliefs about the means of attaining the outcome envisioned. Of course Weber knew perfectly well that many actions are *not* purposively rational, and that some are not rational at all. Yet even for such cases, Weber recommended the model of purposively rational action as a useful starting point, if only to 'measure' the *deviation* between the course of action that *would have been* rational and the behaviors actually observed.[4]

The other trap we must avoid is the temptation to confound the 'subjectivity' of the agents under investigation with the 'subjectivity' of the investigator. Weber distinguished the "inner" processes that define the "sense" or "meaning" *(Sinn)* of an action from the "outer" behaviors that are shaped by that meaning. But he was interested neither in inner states for their own sake nor in mere bodily movements as such. Like Simmel, he avoided the tacit assumption that successful causal explanations must be *microscopic,* linking all *elementary* constituents of a total state to their counterparts in a subsequent state. The cultural and social sciences, he held, deal primarily with the causal *relationships* between "inner" meanings and their "outer" expressions; indeed, a motivational interpretation can be empirically validated only in terms of the outward behaviors it actually accounts for, and these are objectively given.[5]

At no point did Weber suggest, in any case, that the identification of an agent's 'subjective' motive depends in any way upon the 'subjectivity' of the interpreter. On the contrary, following Simmel, Weber repeatedly stressed that one does not have to *be* Caesar to understand him. Much of Weber's commentary on Knies, in fact, was written to challenge the subjectivist fallacy that interpretation is an intuitive 'identification' with the persons who are 'understood,' or an empathetic reproduction of their inner states. Of course we may at times "experience" *(erleben)* an apparently unmediated sense of another person's feelings. Still, we must leave the realm of immediate but inarticulate insight to reach justifiable interpretations,

---

4. Weber, "Knies," pp. 126–130.

5. Ibid., p. 83. For Weber's repudiation of (Stammler's) thesis that only bodily movement, or the physical and physiological, is capable of causal explanation, see Weber, "Nachtrag," pp. 360–361.

which are deliberate constructions, not intuitive flashes. Weber suspected that irrationalist views of interpretation reflect a confusion between the *genesis* of interpretive understandings and their *justification*. For in the cultural and social sciences as in other disciplines, new knowledge often originates in intuitions, which then have to be validated in more formal arguments and procedures.[6]

Weber acknowledged the role of informal, commonsense, or 'folk psychology' *(Vulgärpsychologie)* in what he sometimes called 'empathetic understanding.' He believed that both observed behavioral regularities and forms of 'rational action' may sustain judgments of 'adequate causation' in human affairs. At the same time, he strenuously resisted the view that explanation in the cultural and social sciences must be deduced from the 'laws' of systematic psychology, or that psychology is the foundational science for history, economics, and related disciplines. Psychophysical regularities about responses to stimuli, rote learning and the like, he thought, are mere 'givens' for the historian. Like the findings of the psychopathologist, they may well be causally relevant to singular actions and events. But they function as background conditions, not as elements in interpretations. Historians often draw upon the findings of other disciplines, including the natural sciences; but their primary concern is with the interpretation of actions and beliefs.

> In so far as psychological concepts and rules or statistical data are not accessible to 'interpretation,' they are . . . accepted as 'given,' but . . . do not satisfy . . . [our] specifically 'historical interest.'

This position grew partly out of Weber's identification of the 'historically interesting' with the 'culturally relevant.' But it mainly reflects his conviction that the interpretive explanation of human actions and beliefs is not deducible from psychophysical laws, though it does draw upon 'folk psychology' or, more typically, upon 'rules of rational action.' As Weber wrote in a 1909 letter to Lujo

6. Weber, "Knies," pp. 100, 111–113, 116–122, for this and what follows.

Brentano, "Our 'theory' is 'rational,' not 'psychological,' in its foundations."[7]

Nothing is more central to Weber's methodology, in any case, than the maxim that interpreters must at least *begin* by supposing that the actions and beliefs they seek to understand are 'rational' in some sense of that term. Clearly influenced by Carl Menger's understanding of marginal utility theory as an abstraction from a more complex reality, Weber repeatedly used economic examples to explicate his views. What the "economic principle" stipulates, he argued, is how agents *would* behave if they fully knew their present and future needs, and effectively related them to the resources available to them. Such omniscient and purely rational economic agents may not exist in the real world; but the model is *heuristically* useful, especially in an age of increasing economic rationality. In the same way, we may imagine a perfectly informed and rational military commander, if only to judge to what extent the decisions of an actual general matched those of his ideal colleague. Not only economics, but all the social sciences need such "rational constructions." Economics, especially in its historical form, "interpretively understands human actions in their motives and consequences," and is thus "intimately linked to interpretive sociology."[8]

Weber left no doubt that the rationality he proposed to attribute to the agents and beliefs to be investigated was 'our' rationality, the rationality of the investigator: "We obviously 'understand' without difficulty that a thinker solves a certain 'problem' in a way that we ourselves consider normatively correct." Weber used the term 'right rationality' *(Richtigkeitsrationalität)* to refer to what we (the interpreters) ourselves consider 'correct' reasoning. On the one hand, of course, the norm of 'right rationality' functions as "the a priori of

7. Ibid., pp. 82–84, esp. p. 84. As a behavioral "rule of adequate causation," Weber (p. 112) cited this mock-formal 'lesson' from the German humorist Wilhelm Busch's "Plisch und Plum": "Those who rejoice at others' misfortunes usually make themselves unpopular." Weber noted (a) that this 'rule' could explain British reactions to German attitudes during the Boer War, and (b) that its explicit statement did not add much to our understanding of the particular case it might be said to 'cover.' For the letter to Brentano, see *MWG*, II/6, p. 108.

8. Weber, "Diskussion 1910," pp. 482–483; "Gutachten," pp. 138–139.

all scientific investigation"; but it may also serve more specifically as an aid to interpretive understanding. On the other hand, 'wrong' thinking is accessible to interpretation as well. 'The hypothetical attribution of 'right rationality' to an agent or a text is therefore just an especially useful—and "understandable"—point of departure for the interpretive enterprise.

> Even to 'understand' an incorrect calculation or logical state-ment, and to . . . assess . . . its influence, one not only has to . . . . recheck it by means of correct . . . thinking, but also explicitly to identify . . . the precise point . . . at which [it] deviates from what the [investigator] himself considers 'cor-rect.'

The point of *deviation* may be particularly characteristic, causally relevant or culturally interesting, especially if the "truth value" of a line of reasoning is a source of its 'value relatedness,' as in the history of a discipline. Consistent with his emphasis upon 'right rationality' as a point of departure, Weber insisted that art historians, for example, must be capable of substantive artistic judgments in their own right.[9]

It should be noted that Weber's formulations typically deal with whole patterns or sequences of behavior, rather than with isolated actions. On one occasion, he underlined the causal significance of constant "motives" that, once empirically established, may be as-cribed to a "personality," even while they can be traced in turn to defining experiences and the like. Goethe's letters to Charlotte von Stein, as he pointed out in another passage, are historically interest-ing in their own right; but they may also testify to causal influences upon Goethe's work at that time. They may have been "real links in a causal chain," and even if they had no such immediate impact, they may still offer insights into Goethe's outlook, or into the "intellec-tual habitus" of the circles in which he moved. They could be of interest to a sociologist of culture, or even to a psychiatrist. In short, they may be studied for their own distinctive traits, as means of

9. Weber, "Wertfreiheit," pp. 531–534, 524, esp. pp. 532–533, which closely parallels "Gutachten," pp. 135–136.

insight into surrounding contexts, or as elements in the network of causal chains that make up the historical world. Weber's methodology was highly flexible; it presupposed interpretation; but its overall framework was a dynamic causalism.[10]

In his 1907 essay on Rudolf Stammler, Weber defended his vision of causal analysis against what he clearly considered fashionable obscurantism. Stammler, regarding legal and conventional norms as constitutive of social systems, had characterized group life as essentially 'rule-governed' *(geregelt)*. While holding that his insight undermined 'historical materialism,' he also suggested that the actions of Robinson Crusoe, the hypothetically isolated economic individual, were purely 'technical' and thus objects of investigation for the natural rather than the social sciences. Reacting sharply, Weber pointed out that Robinson's 'techniques' for survival were no more or less decisively affected by his beliefs about the effects of his actions than those of an entrepreneur trying to manage his workers by means of wages and other positive or negative incentives. The fact that the entrepreneur reckons with causal chains that encompass conscious processes, Weber argued, is irrelevant in principle. Of course human actions must be understood in terms of their meanings. But if Crusoe deliberately notches trees that he intends to cut for the winter, his actions are quite as meaningful as the manager's recourse to monetary conventions.[11]

More important, Weber directly attacked the thesis that to understand a society is to grasp the 'rules' that govern it. He did this partly by distinguishing several senses of the word 'rule' *(Regel):* a rule may be an observed *regularity,* one less strict than a scientific law, yet sound enough to sustain a judgment of 'adequate causation'; it may be a legal or customary *norm* of conduct; or it may be a behavioral *maxim,* the 'rule' actually guiding an action. Legal or conventional norms accepted as valid within a social group may nonetheless be circumvented in practice. Furthermore, agents may be partly or wholly unaware of the maxims guiding their behavior, so that only 'outside' investigators can fully articulate them. Thus

10. Weber, "Knies," p. 48; "Studien," pp. 241–244.
11. Weber, "Stammler," esp. pp. 324–326, 331–333.

social scientists cannot be content to understand the 'rules' of a society; they must interpret and explain the actions and beliefs of social agents. Of course juridical laws may function as causes, affecting expectations about the effects of behaviors, especially if they are reinforced by sanctions. For the sociologist, Weber remarked, the 'validity' of a law is just the empirical "chance" that under given circumstances, certain actions—or other consequences—will ensue. Moreover, laws and maxims alike may serve as hypothetical models of social practice, if only to 'measure' the distances that separate them from the observed realities. Investigators themselves may construct such maxims as those of economic rationality for analogous analytical purposes. Still, no matter through what cognitive strategies, social scientists must seek to know the causes and consequences of social actions; their task cannot be limited to the understanding of 'rules' in Stammler's loose sense of that term.[12]

Interpretive Sociology

Among Weber's methodological writings, two stand out as particularly significant, because they summarize Weber's own position without commenting upon the work of others. Their titles, in translation, are "About Some Categories of Interpretive Sociology" (1913), and "Basic Concepts of Sociology" (1921), and the first is really an early version of the second. Taken together, these two articles offer a full and consistent account of Weber's project. They are densely written and hard to read. Yet even at the cost of occasional repetition, we should follow these formulations with close attention.

Here are the well-known definitions that form the opening of the second essay.

Sociology . . . [is] a discipline that seeks interpretively to understand social action and thereby causally to explain it in its progression and in its effects. 'Action' . . . [is defined as] hu-

12. Ibid., pp. 322–324, 328–331, 336–337, 342–343, 356–357; Weber, "Diskussion 1910," p. 478. Even the multiplication table, Weber added in "Wertfreiheit," p. 531, concerns the historical sociologist not as a norm, but as a conventional maxim that affects actions.

man behavior (whether outer or inner) . . . [and including failure to act] in so far as the agent or agents associate it with a subjective meaning. 'Social' action . . . is . . . related in its intended meaning, and oriented in its progression, to the behavior of others.

While the principal subject matter of sociology is thus defined as *social* action, Weber acknowledges that much of the action of interest to the sociologist is oriented toward the nonmeaningful objects of the 'external world.' In fact, he devotes less attention to the obvious distinction between action and *social* action than to the more difficult topic of meaningful action in general. When he writes about the 'progression' *(Verlauf, Ablauf)* of an action, he points not only to behavioral *sequences,* rather than isolated events, but also to the 'outer' manifestations of 'inner' processes. The interpretive sociologist, he specifies, is interested neither in purely inward states nor in outward behavior as such, but in *action,* especially in action that is "co-determined by . . . its meaningful relatedness to the behavior of others and . . . interpretively explainable in terms of . . . [its] intended meaning."[13]

As in other contexts, Weber insists that an action must be understood in terms of the agent's "subjectively intended" meaning, rather than a logically 'valid' or metaphysically 'true' meaning. The investigator must know what the agent or agents really had in mind; what actually made them act as they did. This is what sets the cultural and social studies apart from such prescriptive or dogmatic fields of inquiry as jurisprudence, logic, ethics, or aesthetics. Logical or juridical norms and constructs may serve as hypothetical models in the search for subjectively intended meanings; but that is a question about analytical tactics, not about the objects of study. As for the intended meanings of actions, they may be those of a single individual, those prevailing *on the average* within a particular group, or those attributed to a hypothetically constructed 'typical' agent.

13. Weber, "Grundbegriffe," p. 1; "Kategorien," pp. 431, 429.

'Understanding' . . . signifies the interpretation of the meaning
or complex of meanings (a) actually intended in a particular
case . . . or (b) intended on the average and approximately . . .
or (c) to be constructed . . . for the pure type (ideal type) of a
frequent phenomenon. The concepts and 'laws' posited by
pure economic theory, for example, are such ideal-typical constructions. . . . Real action proceeds only rarely (the stock
exchange)—and even then only approximately—as projected in
the ideal type.

Among other things, this passage introduces us to the concept of
the 'ideal type,' which plays so large and complex a role in Weber's
methodology that we will shortly consider it at greater length. For
the moment, we need to recognize only that the 'pure' economic
theory of Carl Menger informed Weber's account of 'ideal typical'
construction, and that he frequently used the example of economic
theory to clarify the tactics of interpretation.[14]

While charting the concepts and methods of 'interpretive sociology,' Weber repeatedly called attention to the *limits* of interpretive
understanding. Along with pathological states, which may be partly
understandable for experts, he cited such "nonmeaningful" or
"meaningless" *(sinnfremd)* phenomena as the onset of epidemics and
the facts of the human life cycle, such psychophysical processes as
changes in pulse rates or reaction times, rates of rote learning, habitu-
ation, and fatigue, and such 'naked' psychological facts as feelings of
physical pleasure and pain. Discoverable regularities in these areas,
Weber held, are no more closely related to the cognitive objectives of
the cultural and social sciences than the more typical laws of the
natural sciences, including the laws of biology pertinent to epidemics,
for example. Of course, 'meaningless' realities may be of very great
significance as conditions and consequences of human actions.

Nonmeaningful processes or objects are relevant for all disciplines concerned with actions, as occasions, outcomes, aids or

14. Weber, "Grundbegriffe," pp. 1–2, 4, esp. p. 4; see also "Grenznutzlehre,"
pp. 396–397.

impediments of human actions. 'Nonmeaningful' is not identical with 'nonliving' or 'nonhuman.'

For on the one hand, machines can be 'understood' in relation to human purposes and actions, whether as means or as products. On the other hand, human actions are thoroughly integrated into a wider network of causal relationships, which also encompasses 'meaningless' phenomena.[15]

Weber repeatedly tried to chart the range of phenomena that can be interpreted, along with the different types of 'understanding' involved. In a somewhat problematic effort at classification, he suggested a basic distinction between "immediate" *(aktuell)* and "explanatory" understanding.

Understanding can signify (1) the immediate understanding of the intended meaning of an action (including an expression). For example, we immediately 'understand' the meaning of the sentence $2 \times 2 = 4$ that we hear or read (rational immediate understanding of thoughts), or an outburst of anger that manifests itself in facial expressions, interjections, irrational motions (irrational immediate understanding of affects), or the behavior of someone who chops wood or . . . aims a gun at an animal (rational immediate understanding of actions).

But understanding can also signify (2) explanatory understanding. We 'understand' in terms of motives [motivationally] what meaning the person who enunciated or wrote down the sentence $2 \times 2 = 4$ associated with it by doing it just at a certain time and in a certain context, if we see him engaged in . . . an economic calculation . . . [or] a technical assessment, into which the sentence 'fits' and thus takes on a certain meaning . . . (rational understanding of motives). We understand the chopping of wood or the aiming of the gun, not only immediately but also motivationally, if we know that the person chopping wood did so either for pay or . . . for recreation (rationally), or perhaps 'because he was abreacting nervous

15. Weber, "Kategorien," pp. 428–431; "Grundbegriffe," p. 3.

excitement' (irrationally). . . . Finally, we motivationally understand the outburst of anger, if we know that it stems from
jealousy . . . [or] wounded pride (affectually conditioned, and
thus motivationally irrational). All these are understandable
relations of meaning, the understanding of which we consider
explanations for the actual progression of behaviors.[16]

The passage is not only complicated but also confusing—and potentially misleading.

Part of the problem lies in the notion of 'immediate' (or 'current':
aktuell) 'understanding.' The term comes close to suggesting empathetic reproduction, particularly when applied to an emotional
outburst, for example. We know that Weber elsewhere repudiated
subjectivist accounts of 'understanding,' while emphasizing the difference between the genesis of an interpretation and its justification.
To remain consistent with that position, the word *aktuell* can only
signify the more or less instantaneous way in which certain propositions or gestures are 'understood,' presumably on the basis of prior
experience that could be partly or wholly specified. Yet the warrant
for our reconstruction of a mathematical proposition or theorem
surely differs from that for our 'reading' of a facial expression (which
might even be feigned). To defend particular interpretations of such
behaviors surely requires extended analyses of the relevant contexts,
in which the distinction between 'immediate' and 'explanatory'
understanding will tend to break down. This is true also with respect
to such actions as aiming a gun at an animal (or playfully pointing
it, or testing the sights), which can scarcely be understood without
reference to the 'motive'—in all its potential complexity. Weber's
whole catalogue thus really boils down to his early distinction
between the rational reconstruction of 'expressions' (in Simmel's
sense of 'thought contents') and the interpretation of actions, including the action of speaking or writing, in terms of 'motives' that
are causes.

In a more systematic approach to the varieties of 'understanding,'
Weber began by describing possible interpretations as more or less

16. Weber, "Grundbegriffe," pp. 3–4.

"evident." He used the German term *Evidenz* to signify something like verisimilitude. Like all cognition, he argued, interpretation strives for *Evidenz,* which in the case of 'understanding' may be either rational or empathetic. The "rationally evident" is "intellectually understood," fully clarified and penetrated in its "meaning relationships." The "empathetically evident" is "fully reexperienced." Thus, on the one hand, we completely understand the Pythagorean theorem, logically 'right' reasoning, sound inferences from empirical data, or the choice of empirically proven means to attain given ends; it is of course *our* standards that determine what is 'right,' sound, or empirically proven. Somewhat less fully, we understand errors or confusions to which we ourselves might have succumbed. On the other hand, we can empathetically reexperience irrational states, emotional relationships, or sequences of affects only to the extent that we have passed through them ourselves. Weber clearly considered this kind of projection from the interpreter's 'inner' experience much less reliable than rational understanding. Noting again that one does not have to be Caesar to understand Caesar, he argued that the ability to reexperience another's feelings on the basis of one's own is *not* a precondition of understanding as such. It may enhance the *Evidenz* of an interpretation; but the fact that it "possesses this quality of *Evidenz* to a particularly high degree," Weber wrote, "does not . . . in itself prove anything about its empirical validity." "For behaviors identical in their external progression and result may rest upon greatly divergent constellations of motives." Wherever possible, the 'understanding' of a meaning relationship must therefore be "checked with the ordinary methods of causal analysis."[17]

Weber was especially cautious about the role of empathy. Mystical experiences that cannot be articulated, he warned, are bound to be incompletely accessible for interpreters not susceptible to such states. The behaviors of infants are hard to interpret. Ultimate value orientations, as well as sexual and other instinctual drives, are typically not understood, but simply accepted as given. Sociologists must be prepared to deal with merely pretended purposes, rationali-

17. Ibid., p. 2; Weber, "Kategorien," p. 428.

zations, displaced emotional gratifications, and plainly incomprehensible motivations. Meaningful and nonmeaningful elements may be intertwined in a sequence of phenomena, and behaviors may be 'objectively' rational, though the agents involved are unaware of the consistencies observable in their actions.

Weber actually distinguished *four* types of action: in the eyes of the relevant *agents,* "purposively rational [*zweckrational*]" action is 'adequate' to bring about desired ends; "value rational [*wertrational*]" action is grounded in coherent normative commitments; "traditional" action follows accustomed patterns of practice, while "affectual" action is driven by purely emotional states. In his substantive sociological and political writings, Weber repeatedly stressed the differences between these four kinds of behavior, especially that between purposively rational and value rational action. In his methodological essays, however, he mainly emphasized the divide between rationality and irrationality, while assigning a particularly vital role to *purposive* rationality. But he also pointed out that even the line between meaningful action and merely reactive behavior is far from clear in reality; traditional orientations in effect straddle the border between the two realms. It is in the light of these complexities that Weber stressed the need to verify interpretive hypotheses by means of ordinary causal reasoning.[18]

At the same time, Weber firmly anchored the tactics of interpretation in the hypothetical models of *purposive* and of *'right'* rationality. Interpretation based upon the assumption of the agent's purposive rationality, according to Weber, achieves a high degree of *Evidenz.* To suppose that an action was *indeed* purposively rational (from the interpreter's point of view) is to say that certain means *had to be* chosen to reach the ends in view. The model of purposively rational action may thus be linked to the ideal type of 'right rationality' *(Richtigkeitstypus),* which applies to the interpretation of value rational actions and of *beliefs* as well: maximally 'evident' to us is reasoning that meets our own standards of rationality, along with actions and outcomes demonstrably brought about by appropriate

18. Weber, "Kategorien," pp. 429, 433, 435; "Grundbegriffe," pp. 2, 12–13, including for what preceded.

means. Of course we must not *automatically* attribute rationality to a text or to an agent. A tactical construct of action based upon errors of judgment *(Irrtumstypus)* may be just as relevant in a particular instance as the type of right rationality. Even well-established mathematical theorems and logical norms are no more significant for the student of action, in any case, than "conventional usages" that *may* have affected observed behaviors.

> The degree of right rationality of an action is an empirical question. For where the real relationships among their objects are concerned, rather than their own presuppositions, empirical disciplines unavoidably practice 'naive realism,' although in forms that vary with the characteristics of their objects.

It follows that interpretation on the rationality model is a *strategic* device, *not an ultimate goal* of sociology, and that sociology is *not* inherently 'rationalistic.' On the contrary, as Weber strenuously insisted, practitioners of the cultural and social sciences rarely encounter *purely rational* actions and beliefs *in reality*. Their 'rationalism' is exclusively heuristic.[19]

All the more important is the tactical role Weber assigned to observed *deviations* from purposive and/or right rationality. His formulations on this subject recall his triadic scheme of singular causal explanation. Having projected the course of action that *would* follow from purposive rationality, sociologists must chart the *divergence* between it and the actual 'progression' of behavior, since that alone will permit "the causal attribution of the deviation to the irrationalities" that account for it.

> The more clearly an action . . . [conforms to] right rationality, the less . . . [need is there for] psychological considerations. Conversely, any explanation of 'irrational' processes . . . primarily requires the sociologist to determine how the action would have proceeded in the limiting case of purposive and

19. Weber, "Grundbegriffe," p. 1; "Kategorien," pp. 428, 434, 437–438, esp. p. 437.

right rationality. For only . . . [in the light of this determination can the sociologist] undertake the causal attribution of the [behavior] to . . . objectively and subjectively 'irrational' components . . . [or judge] what aspects of the action . . . are 'only psychologically' explicable . . . based upon objectively erroneous orientations, or upon subjectively purposive irrationality . . . [i.e. upon] motives that are either wholly incomprehensible and [thus] knowable only through rules of experience, or else understandable but not purposively rational.

The passage suggests a rich collection of interpretive strategies, from the model of right rationality, to other forms of 'understandably' meaningful or 'psychologically' comprehensible action and belief, and finally on to behaviors that can only be explained by reference to 'rules of experience.'[20]

More specifically, Weber noted that investigators may encounter purposively rational actions based upon assumptions they cannot share; magical practices based upon animist beliefs may serve as examples. In a catalogue of possibilities confronting the interpretive sociologist, Weber distinguished the following six alternatives: (1) the more or less fully realized type of right rationality, (2) the type of subjectively purposive rationality, (3) action more or less unconsciously or incompletely oriented in a purposively rational sense, (4) action that is not purposively rational but understandably meaningful, (5) behavior that is less than fully understandable as meaningful and more or less interspersed or codetermined by nonmeaningful relationships, and (6) wholly incomprehensible psychic or physical states. These six possibilities, according to Weber, are not clearly separated in reality; rather, they are linked by gradual transitions on a single continuous scale.[21]

Nevertheless, Weber was particularly interested in the divergence between the ideal type of right rationality and empirically observed beliefs and behavioral 'progressions.' As in other contexts, he added that both right rationality and deviations from it may be culturally

20. Weber, "Grundbegriffe," p. 2; "Kategorien," pp. 430–432, esp. p. 432.
21. Ibid., pp. 433, 435.

as well as causally significant, depending upon the investigator's value-related concerns: "Not only for a history of logic or of other disciplines, but in all other areas as well . . . [the] seams at which tensions between the empirical and the type of right rationality can break open are of the highest significance." One clear instance of the tension Weber refers to is that between rational reconstruction and attention to empirical contingency in the history of knowledge.[22]

It is the tactical centrality of right rationality in interpretation that accounts for Weber's reservations about psychology. He admitted that the understanding of irrational states may be facilitated by certain forms of interpretive psychology, including 'folk' psychology. He further conceded that truly significant behavioral laws may eventually be discovered. Yet even if that happens, Weber believed, the enhanced science of psychology will be no more fundamental to the enterprise of interpretation than the findings of biology, for example. Above all, such models as that of economically rational action are applicable to individuals of divergent 'psychological' characteristics. Too many methodologists simply *assume* that what is not 'physical' must be 'psychological.' Yet "the meaning of a mathematical problem is surely not 'psychological'"—on these grounds, Max Weber was no less hostile than Emile Durkheim to the notion that psychology is the theoretical foundation of sociology.[23]

At the same time, Weber was extremely cautious about the reliability of interpretation itself. In his deliberately broad definition, a motive is a meaning relation that is taken to be a "reason" *(Grund)* for an action. But as he repeatedly pointed out, motives may be feigned, mixed, unacknowledged, or actually unconscious. More generally, a highly 'evident' interpretation, one that is unquestionably "adequate at the level of meaning," may nevertheless be causally "inadequate." Thus a plausible motivational interpretation can never be more than a promising hypothesis about the real cause of an action—until it is checked against the relevant 'progression' of external behaviors. An adequate interpretation, one could say, is a

---

22. Ibid., pp. 433, 438, footnote 1.
23. Ibid., pp. 430, 432, and esp. "Grundbegriffe," p. 9.

necessary but not a sufficient condition for the adequate explanation of an action. In the case of group actions, statistical data may help to confirm the causal adequacy of a meaningful interpretation, even though a statistical regularity cannot, by itself, satisfy our need for a causal understanding of actions. Comparative analysis, too, may aid us in identifying reasons that are causally as well as meaningfully adequate. Otherwise, our only recourse is to counterfactual analysis, in which we hypothetically delete a portion of a motivational chain and 'construct' the probable sequence of external behaviors in its absence. Though aware of the great difficulties involved, Weber nonetheless saw 'understandable' meaning relationships, and especially purposively rational motivations, as crucial elements in the cultural and social sciences. Indeed, he described reasons or motives as potential "links in a causal chain" that "begins in external circumstances and ultimately terminates again in outward behaviors." Sociology, as he concluded, "would have to protest against the assumption that 'understanding' and causal 'explanation' have no relationship to each other."[24]

The Ideal Type and Its Functions

Weber's methodology, and especially his theory of interpretation, can scarcely be imagined apart from his concept of the 'ideal type.' We know that this concept was at least partly inspired by Carl Menger, and that Weber persistently cited neoclassical economic theory to illustrate the uses of 'ideal-typical' construction. Another potential source of Weber's typological approach was the work of the legal and political theorist Georg Jellinek, one of Weber's friends. Jellinek noted that the social sciences lack the strict causal laws and empirical regularities characteristic of the natural sciences. He traced the difference to the role of "qualitative" factors, of human agents and, more generally, of "individualizing elements" in human affairs. He criticized the "natural law" tradition in political theory because it depended upon universal generalizations unrelated to the study of real or "positive" law. Nevertheless, he believed that

24. Ibid., pp. 4–5; "Kategorien," pp. 436–437.

political science should attend not only to the distinctive characteristics of particular institutions, but to "typical" patterns as well. In that context, Jellinek defined the "ideal type" of the political state as a "teleological" norm, a standard of perfection that could be used to assess actually existing states. He added, however, that the social sciences are primarily concerned with *what is,* and not with *what ought to be.* Although he regarded the "average type" as the "antithesis" of the "ideal type," he recommended the "inductive" establishment of "types" based upon commonalities among sufficiently similar political systems. Carefully limited generalizations about such "types," he thought, might have a certain predictive force, while also helping to point up the distinctive traits of particular states. Obviously, there *are* parallels between Jellinek's and Weber's conceptions. Yet Weber surely owed more to Menger than to Jellinek, even though Jellinek may be said to have *named* the "ideal type."[25]

Weber himself first extensively discussed the "ideal type" in his 1904 essay on "Objectivity." As usual, his point of departure was "abstract economic theory," which can provide an "ideal portrait" of the processes resulting from "strictly rational action" in a competitive "free market" economy. This "construction" has a "utopian" character, in that it is obtained by conceptually "heightening" certain aspects of reality. Where we suspect the empirical presence of relationships resembling those emphasized in the "ideal type," the 'type' can help us to "understand" and to "portray" these connections. It can also guide our causal attributions; though *not itself a hypothesis,* it may *suggest* fruitful hypotheses. Among further examples of 'ideal types,' Weber mentioned the "idea" of "the medieval urban economy," or of "artisanal," as opposed to modern "capitalist," production. In these cases too, certain aspects of reality may be "one-sidedly exaggerated," and historical research assigned the task of determining to what extent realities deviated from their abstract portrait. 'Ideal types' are not normatively exemplary, of course; they are "pure constructs of relationships" that we conceive as "sufficiently motivated," "objectively probable" and thus causally

25. Jellinek, *Allgemeine Staatslehre,* pp. 25–39.

"adequate" in the light of our "nomological knowledge." They are valuable as cognitive *means*, to the extent that they lead to knowledge of "concrete cultural phenomena in their interconnections, their causes, and their significance."[26]

The deliberate construction of ideal types, Weber thought, must seem problematic to those who see historical scholarship as a 'reproduction' of the past, a summation of "objective facts" that is free of all "presuppositions." Yet as soon as historians begin to replace informal descriptions of "individualism" or "feudalism" with more precise definitions, they are bound to find themselves forming constructs and "limiting concepts" that isolate significant aspects of the realities they hope to penetrate. Their need for this tactic will increase if they seek a *genetic* understanding of such phenomena as that of the religious "sect," for example, since they must then imagine adequate *causal* relationships between certain forms of sectarian spirituality and significant characteristics of modern culture. The more rigorously they specify these relationships, of course, the less likely are their 'utopias' to 'match' the inchoate complexities of the empirical world.[27]

Still, as Weber insisted, the line between the ideal type and reality must not be blurred. Thus cultural and social scientists must strenuously avoid two fallacies that Weber traced to "naturalist" or essentialist assumptions. One of these is the error of equating their own constructs with the "essence" of the historically given, as if real phenomena could be "deduced" from these constructs. The other, more dangerous temptation is to "hypostatize" the historian's "ideas," making them generative "forces" that are somehow 'realized' in the historical process. This fallacy is particularly seductive, since the historian's ideal type of an age or culture often refers to attitudes, beliefs, and ideals of *participants* in that age or culture. In the face of these complexities, investigators urgently have to distinguish between *their* constructs of social and institutional patterns, *their* 'heightened' portraits of historical beliefs and attitudes, *their* ideal types of the interrelationships between sociopolitical environments and ideas, and the *real* worlds, beliefs, and attitudes of the

26. Weber, "Objektivität," pp. 190–193.
27. Ibid., pp. 193–195.

historical agents they hope to understand. In order to emphasize the divide between the historian's constructs and the empirically given, Weber pointed to agents who are incompletely conscious of their motives, although the 'outside observer' can detect and account for the maxims implied in their practices. For good measure, he noted that it is not the "logic" of a doctrine (e.g. 'predestination') that affects actions, but its "psychological" impact upon a particular group of agents (e.g. Protestant sectarians).[28]

While most ideal types address the relationships among particulars, according to Weber, some may help to clarify whole classes of phenomena. A merely descriptive classification of economic "exchanges," for example, may be turned into an ideal type of "exchange," if it is linked with marginal utility theory. It will then function as an 'ideal' model of economic action that also has "genetic" implications, since it hypothetically traces the behaviors of agents to purposively rational considerations. Most of the concepts of theoretical economics, Weber held, are ideal-typical elaborations upon initially descriptive classifications. Indeed, ideal constructs may be not only "genetic," but "dynamic" in character. To imagine the medieval economy as ideal-typically "artisanal," for instance, is to suppose that its subsequent transformation had to travel along certain well-delimited paths. If we observe that post-medieval economic change in reality *departed* from these paths, we may conclude that the medieval economy was *not* strictly "artisanal," and we may begin to understand how and why it diverged from the "artisanal" model. Weber believed that the Marxist "laws" of capitalist development were dynamic ideal types—and very fruitful ones, as long as they were not submerged in "naturalist" assumptions. Furthermore, Weber did *not* regard ideal types as temporary props for an immature field of inquiry. Rather, he expected them to remain permanent features of the cultural and social sciences, if only because they were partly shaped by the changing cultural interests of investigators in these disciplines.[29]

What really strikes me about Weber's ideal type, however, is its tactical role in an analytical strategy that rests upon Weber's triadic

28. Ibid., pp. 195–200.
29. Ibid., pp. 200–206.

model of singular causal analysis. The ideal type is deliberately constructed to project a hypothetical 'progression' of external behaviors that *could be* fully explained in terms of understandable 'motives' (and beliefs about means conducive to the ends in view). In the analysis of virtually all *real* actions, such ideal-typical projections become secure—though *counterfactual*—bases for the causal ascription of *deviations* from the rationally understandable 'progression' to *divergences* between the 'motivations' stipulated in the type and those actually moving the agents involved.

Let us consider two particularly revealing formulations on this subject.

> The rational construction [of an ideal general's decisions] . . . functions as a means of causal 'attribution.' Exactly the same purpose is served by those utopian constructions of error-free and rigorously rational action that are created by 'pure' economic theory. . . . Logically considered, however, the construction of such a rationally 'right' utopia is only one of the various forms of an 'ideal type.' . . . Normatively 'right' [action] has no monopoly in this respect. For whatever content the ideal type is given . . . its only value . . . for empirical investigations lies in its purpose: to 'compare' empirical reality with it, so as to ascertain . . . the distance or degree of approximation between [reality and the type], and thus to be able to describe and causally to explain [reality] in terms of clearly understandable concepts.

Once again, neoclassical economic theory serves as a prime example of ideal-typical construction. The overall aim is to reach optimally clarified concepts. Empirical action is expected to diverge more or less radically from the rationally understandable course predicted by the ideal type. The 'utopian' construct therefore serves mainly as a *counterfactual* projection, which facilitates the causal ascription of *deviations* from it to 'motives' other than those attributed to the ideal agent.[30]

30. Weber, "Wertfreiheit," pp. 534–536.

Although the rational agent provides a starting point for the investigator who constructs interpretive types, Weber clearly considered other possibilities, as in the following sentence.

> Right rationality serves [interpretive sociology] as an ideal type with respect to empirical action; purposive rationality [plays an analogous role] with respect to . . . meaningfully understandable [action, and] meaningfully understandable [action] with respect to not meaningfully understandable action, by comparison with which [type] the causally relevant irrationalities (in the respectively different senses of the term] can be ascertained for the purpose of causal attribution.

The analytical strategies suggested by these formulations are certainly complex; they call for stepwise approaches to reality by means of increasingly fruitful interpretive constructs. In its underlying structure, however, the typological approach closely parallels Weber's triadic scheme of singular causal explanation.[31]

Figure 3 is a graphic representation of ideal-typical analysis, which really duplicates the illustration of singular causal argument in Figure 1.

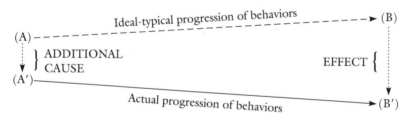

Figure 3

The dashed line (A-B) stands for the external 'progression' of behaviors that *would have* occurred if the agent had acted as stipulated in the ideal type. The line (A'-B') is the actually observed progression of behaviors. The positing of the ideal type allows the investigator to 'compare' (A'-B') with (A-B) and thus to 'measure'

31. Weber, "Kategorien," p. 436.

the *deviation* (B-B′) that must be causally attributed to the *differ-ence* between (A), the 'motives' hypothetically ascribed to the ideal-typical agent, and (A′), the 'motivation' of the real agent or agents involved. Note that the diagram represents only one step in what may become a more extended analytical sequence. For the investi-gator may begin by positing an ideal-typical agent whose action was entirely motivated by 'right rationality.' Having found that this supposition falls too far short of accounting for the observed pro-gression of behaviors, however, the investigator may next stipulate a purposively rational agent who drew upon identifiably false or vacuous assumptions, or upon other 'meaningfully understandable' considerations. In principle, the investigator must supplement the 'motives' ascribed to the ideal-typical agent until the behaviors projected on that basis 'match' those actually observed. This aim must be maintained even if it ultimately requires partial or total recourse to irrational causes of action. The investigator *must* be able to deal with antecedents of action that range over the whole scale from 'rightly rational' reasons to utterly meaningless causes. Indeed, this strategic imperative strengthens the case for Weber's assump-tion that the interpretation of action is a form of singular causal analysis.

The centrality of rational interpretation for Weber's analytical strategy was first emphasized by Dieter Henrich more than forty years ago. The chief function of the 'ideal type,' according to Henrich, is to specify the hypothetical attribution of rationality to historical agents. Once clearly identified as heuristic constructs, the models of right and purposive rationality serve the interpretive enterprise as points of departure and frameworks of causal ascrip-tion. Against the identificationist view of 'understanding' as an empathetic reproduction, the 'ideal typical' method exposes the *active* role of the investigator in the interpretive process. In positing rational actions and beliefs, moreover, it commits interpreters to a broader project of rational clarification. Cultural and social scientists *begin*, in effect, by inquiring into potentially rational grounds of action and belief. Even if they recognize that the empirical 'expres-sions' and behaviors they encounter are not rationally grounded, they continue to look for—and to articulate—*possibly relevant* relationships of meaning. They may thus tend to understate the degree to which practices are unreflected or unconsciously motivated. Yet this risk is outweighed by the advantages of a fully explicit relationship to one's own motives and beliefs, as well as to those one seeks to understand. Like other coherent visions of interpretation, Weber's theory implied an interaction between self-knowledge (or knowledge of one's own culture) and the understanding of others (or of other cultures). In Weber's case, the rational clarification of motives and beliefs was linked to the ideal of the self-conscious and autonomous "personality."[32]

More critical of Weber's theory of interpretation than Henrich is W. G. Runciman, whose perspective recalls that of C. G. Hempel. Runciman argues that Weber overstated the differences between the natural and the social sciences. In the natural sciences too, as Runciman points out, the cultural interests of investigators may affect the selection of problems for study, and the laws of the natural sciences too may be 'ideal-typical.' But while Weber was aware of these parallels, he still saw differences of *degree* between the two groups of disciplines. A physical law, for instance, is not simply identical with a Weberian 'ideal type.' While sometimes plainly affected by the cultural interests of investigators, moreover, the natural sciences are nevertheless more often guided by established research programs than the singular analyses of the cultural and social sciences. Runciman's main objection, in any case, is directed against Weber's view that the explanations of the cultural and social sciences cannot be deduced from the 'laws' of psychology. Although Runciman admits that we know few if any relevant psychological 'laws,' he believes that the explanations put forward by social scientists depend *in principle* upon "presumptive general grounding at a different level," including that of a foundational psychology. But while this thesis is hard to refute, it is equally hard to accept *in practice*. If, on the one hand, the reference to 'presumptive general grounding' is taken to imply a commitment to Hempel's 'covering law model' in its 'deductive-nomological' form, then it seems largely irrelevant to the *specifics*

32. Henrich, *Wissenschaftslehre.*

of Weber's account of singular causal analysis. If the call for 'presumptive grounding' is interpreted broadly enough, on the other hand, then it is satisfactorily answered by Weber's occasionally explicit recourse to loosely 'nomological' knowledge. In either case, Runciman's objection seems oddly disengaged from the analytical tactics Weber actually recommended.[33]

A 1989 paper by Wolfgang Mommsen is helpful as a corrective to Runciman, in that it reflects a fuller engagement with the relevant texts. Yet it remains misleading in decisive respects. Contrasting Weber's methodology with 'logical positivism,' Mommsen rightly notes that the concept of the 'ideal type' permits Weber to join interpretation to explanation. Mommsen further observes that Weber's ideal-typical analysis is equally applicable to individual behaviors and to broader patterns of meaning and action. Indeed, it provides a basis for the analysis not only of isolated and static phenomena but also of cultural systems, historical structures, and long-term developments. We will certainly have to come back to these fruitful observations in Chapter 6. But Mommsen's commentary also raises two serious problems. First, he argues that the later and more systematic (1913 and 1920) statements of Weber's position reveal a change of emphasis from the concept of the 'ideal type' to that of the 'pure type,' and he links this shift to a tension between Weber's models of 'right rationality' and of 'subjectively motivated' action. The difficulty is that neither the relevant distinctions nor the decisive textual examples are fully specified. Second and more important, Mommsen takes a highly problematic view of Weber's ideal type that is apparently shared by others as well. Since the type is *not* a hypothesis, according to this view, it can be constructed in an essentially gratuitous way, without regard for realities, and guided only by the cultural 'perspectives' of investigators. But this is surely

---

33. Runciman, *Critique,* esp. p. 78. Runciman rightly challenges Weber's distinction between "current" *(aktuell)* and "explanatory" understanding; he also distrusts Weber's 'value interpretation,' which will be discussed in the next chapter. He believes, finally, that Weber really meant to stress the need for preliminary *descriptions* of the cultural attitudes and beliefs that social scientists seek to explain. But this ignores precisely what interested Weber, namely, the *interpretive* strategies required to reach such 'descriptions.'

a misjudgment. Weber's concept of the ideal type just cannot be rightly understood *apart from his broader strategies* of singular and interpretive causal analysis.[34]

A brief summary of these strategies may reinforce the point: to interpret a text or an action, according to Weber, we begin by assuming that it is (or was) rational in the light of our own relevant criteria ('rightly rational'). We then check whether the actual sequence of sentences in the text—or of observed behaviors—is (or was) consistent with this initial assumption. To the extent that we observe inconsistencies, we introduce supplementary hypotheses: perhaps an understandable error was made; or assumptions were involved that are interpretably 'meaningful' but not rational in our sense. Alternately, we may be dealing with unreflected 'beliefs' or 'traditional' actions, which must be traced to inherited institutions or practices. Or irrational attitudes may be involved that are best deduced from empirical 'rules' of commonsense 'psychology.' This is just a partial list of the possibilities. Weber named others; he did not try to exhaust the alternatives, and he insisted that the borderlines between the options were imprecise in any case. What he mainly conveyed was the vision of a *hierarchy* of interpretive constructions that *begins* with the hypothesis of 'right rationality,' extends through a spectrum of more or less 'meaningful' actions and beliefs, and ends in the realm of the purely irrational. Consistent with his view that interpretation is a form of causal analysis, Weber saw the explanation of irrational behaviors as the endpoint of a continuum that also encompasses meaningful action. To imagine his overall scheme, one has to conceive observed incongruities from initially posited lines of interpretation as *deviations* from expected paths in the sense of the diagrams that have been presented.

Understood in this context, Weber's 'ideal type' has three main functions. First, it spells out the stages in the process of interpretation, along with the broader strategy of causal analysis. In a theoretically heightened form, it demonstrates how the several elements

---

34. Mommsen, "Ideal Type," pp. 121–132. As Mommsen knows, Weber repeatedly equated the 'ideal' and the 'pure' type.

in a sequence of behaviors may be ascribed to the various factors within the complex of causally relevant motives, beliefs, and other conditions. Second and more specifically, it allows interpreters to articulate the *relationships of meaning* they take to be involved in particular actions or texts. One has to remember that Weber deliberately distinguished the 'adequacy' of an interpretation *at the level of meaning* from the 'adequacy' of a singular causal claim as a whole. A plausible *(evident)* account of a meaning relation, he held, was a necessary but not sufficient condition of a valid explanation in the realm of action. This suggests that the meaning relation alleged by an interpreter should be fully articulated in an ideal type, and thus separated from the empirical procedures necessary to assess its applicability to an observed sequence of behaviors. Third and finally, the 'ideal-typical' approach emphasizes the active role of the investigator in the interpretation of actions and beliefs. Against the illusion of empathetic reproduction, it highlights the engagement of the interpreter's own norms of 'right rationality.' It also portrays the interpretive process as a complex *interaction* between the conceptual world of the investigators and that of the agents and texts they seek to understand. Such intellectual interactions are likely to clarify the interpreters' relationships to their own cultures, even while confronting them with other possibilities. Interpretation may thus have certain broadly educative effects that are distantly related to the German ideal of *Bildung*.[35]

Still, even if all that is clear, we are left with a number of unanswered questions. As Mommsen and others have pointed out, Weber dealt with more than individual actions and single events, and he typically offered more comparative arguments than counterfactual claims. But how was he able to do these things in the light of his methodological prescriptions? How did he manage to engage in the analysis of whole sociocultural patterns, of broad structural changes, and of long-term historical developments? What, in short, was the relationship between his methodological writings and his

---

35. For a theory of education as interpretation, see Ringer, *Fields of Knowledge*, pp. 314–323.

practice as a comparative historian and sociologist? Since I take these questions to be both difficult and important, I propose to discuss them at some length in Chapter 6. But first, I want to take up a final topic in Weber's methodological work itself, and that is the issue of 'objectivity' and value neutrality.

OBJECTIVITY AND VALUE NEUTRALITY

5

What Weber wrote about 'objectivity' and 'value neutrality' in the cultural and social sciences is all too often misconstrued, and yet his formulations are not elusive. To analyze them, I propose (1) to distinguish his partial adaptation of Rickert's philosophy from his contribution to a significant debate within the Social Policy Association, and (2) to separate his relevant writings between 1904 and 1910 from his more systematic statements of 1913 and afterward. Part of my point is that his interest in the problems raised by Rickert declined sharply after 1906 and played virtually no role in his later works. Nevertheless, we should begin by considering both major components of Weber's position through 1910, including his adaptation of Rickert.

The Two Components of Weber's Position through 1910

Weber came closest to Rickert's doctrines in his distinction between 'law-seeking sciences' *(Gesetzeswissenschaften)* and 'sciences of reality' *(Wirklichkeitswissenschaften)*. Interested in singular phenomena and unable to reproduce them in their totality, cultural and social scientists need criteria to select and delimit their objects of study.

> There is no purely 'objective' scientific analysis of cultural or . . . 'social phenomena,' independent of particular and 'one-sided' perspectives, according to which they are . . . selected . . . [and defined]. The reason lies in the . . . cognitive aim

of social scientific projects. . . . We want to understand reality
. . . in its distinctiveness—the interconnectedness and the cultural significance of its particular phenomena in their contemporary form . . . and the grounds of their having
historically become thus-and-not-otherwise.

The *purely* 'objective' analysis that Weber here repudiates is the
misconception of knowledge as a reproduction of the world. The
term 'objective' appears in quotation marks. The argument is that
the objects of the cultural and social sciences, being singular, are
selected and articulated in the light of their cultural significance, and
explained in historical or causal terms. Following Rickert in this
respect, Weber believed that some phenomena are significant primarily for their *causal* relevance to other, 'value related' particulars.
But this still leaves a need for 'one-sided perspectives' to guide the
choice and description of objects that are significant *primarily* in
their relationship to contemporary cultural commitments.[1]

In short, the constructs of the cultural and social sciences reflect
the values of the investigators; they do not emerge from a passively
observed reality. But if that is true, then the 'objectivity' of these
disciplines can only lie in the fact that their inquiries, though "oriented toward . . . value ideas," do not and cannot "prove the
validity" of the values involved. Our cultural concerns *launch* our
investigations; but once at work on a set of phenomena, Weber
argued, we should analyze our evidence for its own sake, without
further regard for our value interests.

Nevertheless, at some point there is a change in the atmos-
phere: the significance of unreflectively applied perspectives
becomes uncertain; the path is lost in the dusk. The light of the
great cultural problems has moved on. Then science too pre-
pares to change its viewpoint and its conceptual apparatus.

The last three sentences are often cited and sometimes overinterpreted. What they show is that Weber accepted and even valued the

---

1. Weber, "Objektivität," pp. 170–171.

energizing impact of contemporary concerns upon the cultural and social sciences. They may also signal how he viewed the crisis of the humanistic disciplines in Germany around the turn of the century—and his own role in it. They do *not* make him a 'subjectivist' in the general sense of that term.[2]

Weber did not, like Rickert, envision the prospect of universal norms of the culturally valuable or value related. He simply conceded the 'subjectivity' of the personal or collective interests that shape the investigators' perspectives. This was consistent with his cultural pluralism, but of course it made portions of Rickert's philosophy irrelevant to his work. At the same time, Weber found it fruitful to investigate potential objects of the cultural and social sciences for their *possible* relationships to contemporary cultural values. That is what he meant by "value interpretation" or "analysis" *(wertbeziehende Interpretation, Wertanalyse)*. Such analysis may serve to articulate the relevance of singular phenomena for our values; but it may also be merely "dialectical," exposing the *conceivable* value relations of cultural objects. Thus our understanding of a particular text or institution might initially be vague and *unconsciously* affected by personal commitments. 'Value analysis' would then transform our inchoate appreciations into explicit judgments of value relatedness. It would clarify the grounds of our interest in certain objects, if only to separate those grounds from the causal analysis of these phenomena.[3]

In his 1906 critique of Eduard Meyer, Weber related his conception of value analysis to the German tradition of *Bildung* on the one hand, and to ordinary historical explanation on the other. Approaching such sources as Goethe's letters to Charlotte von Stein, the Sermon on the Mount, or Marx's *Capital,* we might ask ourselves about the relationship of their 'intellectual contents' to our values. Even if we do not share the commitments they articulate, our engagement with them will tend to broaden our "intellectual horizons" and enhance our "inner life," our "sensitivity to value orientations." Weber's account of this prospect was consistent not only

2. Ibid., p. 213, and esp. p. 214.
3. Weber, "Knies," pp. 122–125; see also "Studien," p. 246.

with his sense of the *interaction* between interpretation and self-understanding, but also with a sophisticated version of the theory of self-development through textual interpretation. At the same time, Weber saw 'value analysis' as a step toward a more complete, historical, and causal explanation. In partial agreement with Meyer, he postulated an initially "substantive," unhistorical reading of a text, one that naively locates it in the interpreter's intellectual field, rather than in its original context. Yet he also insisted that such a reading is a mere preliminary to a more properly historical analysis.

> Obviously, the kind of 'interpretation' we have here termed 'value analysis' is the introductory guide to that other, 'historical' i.e. causal 'interpretation.' The former analysis pointed up the 'valued' elements of the object, the causal 'explanation' of which is the problem of the latter; the former defined the starting points for the causal analysis, and thus provided the crucial perspectives, without which it would lose itself in an uncharted infinity.

Weber left no doubt that a text can be fully understood only in the cultural context that actually shaped it. His distinction between 'value analysis' and historical interpretation is thus purely theoretical and even artificial. But he apparently felt a need for a *logical* divide between the grounds of an interpreter's interest in certain objects and the methods involved in its contextual interpretation and causal explanation.[4]

In any case, it would be an error to see Weber as a cultural relativist. While conceding the 'subjectivity' of the value preferences that affect the selection and delimitation of subject matters, he repeatedly and explicitly stressed the 'objectivity' of research *results* in the cultural and social sciences.

> Unquestionably, the value ideas [that make us decide what is worth investigating] are 'subjective.' . . . And of course they are historically changeable. . . . But . . . it does *not* follow that

4. Weber, "Studien," pp. 246–253, esp. p. 251.

research in the cultural sciences can only have results that are 'subjective' in the sense that they are valid for some people and not for others. What changes, rather, is the degree to which they *interest* some people and not others. In other words: what becomes an object of research, and how far the investigation extends into the infinity of causal connections, that is determined by the value ideas that dominate the researcher and . . . shape his constructs. In the use of these constructs, however, the researcher is bound . . . by the norms of thought. For only that is scientific truth which *wants* to be valid for all who *want* [to know] the truth.

   A methodically correct . . . demonstration in the social sciences, to attain its objective, must be acknowledged as correct by a Chinese as well . . . [and so must] the logical analysis of an ideal . . . even though [the Chinese] may reject the ideal itself.

These passages leave no doubt that Weber *meant* to draw a sharp line between the 'subjective' grounding of the questions raised in the cultural and social sciences and the 'objectivity' of what adequate answers are actually found.[5]

The only path left open to the persistent relativist, therefore, is to argue that Weber's distinction between subjectively motivated problem definitions and objective research results *cannot* be as consistently maintained as he wanted to believe. He admitted, after all, that the value orientations of investigators enter into the very *constitution* of their objects, setting the boundaries of their topics and defining their concepts. How could he expect the 'Chinese' to acknowledge the validity of answers to questions that he could not fully understand or find significant, and that might strike him as misleading or badly put? Those who insist upon reading Weber in this way too easily overlook his belief in the possibility of interpretation *across* cultural differences. They also forget that the ideal constructs he envisaged could be *adjusted* to optimize the analysis of realities he explicitly approached as a 'naive empiricist.'

5. Weber, "Objektivität," pp. 183–184, 155.

In any case, there can be no doubt about what Weber *took away* from his early reflections on the role of cultural interests in the selection and delimitation of research problems. While subjective judgments do enter into our decisions about what is worth knowing, he argued at scholarly conferences in 1909 and 1910, they should not affect our research itself.

> When we consider an 'interesting' fact as empirical scientists, then the question of why it is interesting lies behind us. . . . And even the parties that are in conflict over [value-related policy questions] have an interest in there being someone who says: I do not say that you are right or wrong; I cannot say that with the means of empirical science; instead, I can tell you: these are the facts . . . these are the consequences of things being what they are. Thus if what you want were to happen, then you would have to put up with these or those means and these or those side effects.

The emphasis upon policy disagreements in the passage is symptomatic, since certain debates within the Social Policy Association did at least as much to shape Weber's views on objectivity as the problems initially raised by Rickert.[6]

In 1904, in fact, Werner Sombart, Max Weber, and Edgar Jaffe took over as editors of the *Archiv für Sozialwissenschaft und Sozialpolitik*, the former *Archiv für soziale Gesetzgebung und Statistik*. Supporting Sombart, Weber helped to shape the joint introductory statement by the new editors, and his own essay on "Objectivity" was written to enlarge upon that statement. Indeed, the joint declaration itself called for a clearer distinction between social science and value judgment. The editors recalled that the Social Policy Association was founded to study and recommend reforms within a capitalist framework. Its members repudiated the claim that economic 'laws' could be deduced from the predictably self-interested behavior of economic agents. Some German historical economists did believe in 'laws' of economic development; others were swayed

6. Weber, "Diskussion 1909," p. 420, and esp. "Diskussion 1910," p. 482.

by looser forms of historicism, ethical evolutionism, or cultural relativism, and all were deeply committed to interventionist policies. As a result, many of them came to disregard the divide between the empirically real and the ethically desirable, between what is *(das Seiende)* and what ought to be *(das Seinsollende):* they tried to derive 'scientific' prescriptions from the empirically given. But this is logically impossible. An age that has eaten from the tree of knowledge, Weber wrote, must acknowledge that ideals are human creations; values cannot be 'read off' from the realities around us. To be sure, certain axioms or categories of ethical argument may be universally valid; but they do not suffice to dictate full-bodied cultural ideals or action orientations in specific situations. We are thus inevitably confronted with competing cultural values—and with ideals that are as holy to others as ours are to us.[7]

Weber particularly disliked the idea that socioeconomic policies can be 'scientifically' grounded in an ethical common ground or 'happy medium,' a consensus that excludes only extreme positions. He explicitly attributed this convenient but questionable position to Gustav Schmoller, the influential leader of the younger historical school of economics. Weber clearly disagreed with Schmoller on substantive issues as well. He deeply disliked the bureaucratic paternalism favored by Schmoller and others; but a full discussion of that issue belongs in another context. As a methodologist and a co-editor of the *Archiv,* Weber urged a rigorous divide between social scientific findings and value judgments, along with the fullest possible discussion of both. He certainly did not recommend indifference to policy questions; indeed, he welcomed the energy of passionate commitments. He believed that explicit value preferences could and should be examined for their logical coherence, their relationship to other possible ideals, and their grounding in ultimate value axioms. He suspected that the superficial consensus on policy questions pursued by Schmoller would not survive full examination and debate. And finally, as he insisted again and again, the social sciences *can* provide reliable answers to causal questions. The objective social

7. Weber, "Objektivität," pp. 149–155, 157–159, for this and the following paragraph.

scientist is able to identify the probable consequences of particular policies, along with potentially *undesirable* side effects or ancillary means to the ends in view.

In 1909 Weber reviewed a book by the economist Adolf Weber that seemed to second the call for a separation between science and value judgment. Adolf Weber suggested a reconciliation between the entrepreneurs and the academic champions of social reform, in which the ethically motivated prescriptions of academics were adjusted in the light of the economic 'realities' *(das Seiende)* confronted by businessmen. Adolf Weber claimed that a more realistic science of economics could educate the nation "beyond the limits of partisan politics," dispelling the misconception of an inevitable antagonism between capital and labor, and showing that wage levels depend upon productivity. In response, Max Weber observed that the antagonism between capital and labor was not only a matter of wages. At the same time, he expressly identified himself with the Socialists of the Lectern, who were united in opposition to the Manchesterite dogma that economic policy must follow from purely economic 'realities,' as Adolf Weber implied. Moreover, Max Weber deeply distrusted the supposed exclusion of 'party political' positions.

> The . . . rejection of partisan political positions . . . [only] . . . aggravates the situation, by fostering the illusion that such a contradiction in terms as an 'impartial' judgment could ever be meaningful, or that such ambiguous terms as 'the interests of the whole' or the 'general welfare' could ever be less 'subjective' than any party slogan, no matter how extreme!

Sensing the danger of a new scientistic economism, Weber called for intellectually 'radical' debate.[8]

In floor discussions at the 1909 meeting of the Social Policy Association, Weber joined Werner Sombart in urging a clearer distinction between social science and value judgment. His repeated interventions were deliberately provocative—and unpopular. The

---

8. Weber, "Aufgaben," pp. 616–618, esp. p. 618.

concept of national wealth or welfare *(Volkswohlstand),* he said at one point, is loaded with value implications. It can be more precisely defined as the per capita income of a social grouping; but that could still entail a preference for an economic unit made up of a few rich landowners and a larger number of dependent shepherds over one composed of independent farmers. And what if large agrarian producers destroy some of their crops to maximize their monetary returns? We must avoid concepts that tacitly intermingle scientific and value questions; for such intermingling is "an affair of the devil." Of course we should discuss the logical coherence of value preferences and their possible interdependence. As social scientists, we might be able to convict policy opponents of inconsistency, or of risking unfavorable side effects they have not fully faced. There is nothing unscientific or futile about intensive controversy over policy questions. What must be avoided is only the confounding of logical or empirical claims with value judgments, and the justification of complex measures in terms of ambiguous standards of "productivity," not to mention "average" valuations.[9]

Indeed, the critical examination of "average judgments" seemed to Weber a significant task of the social sciences: "Not that I underestimate [the importance of] value questions; on the contrary: . . . I cannot bear [to see] . . . the weightiest problems that can move a human heart . . . being turned into technically economic questions of 'productivity.'" The Social Policy Association, Weber repeated, had always insisted upon the relevance of noneconomic causes of human action; but it had ended by permitting the confusion of scientific with normative issues. Both science and practice would surely benefit from a reaffirmation of the relevant distinctions.

> And if we have to recognize with a certain regret that among ourselves too, differences in value judgments have become greater than they used to be, then honesty demands that we openly acknowledge the fact. We do not know of any demonstrable ideals.

9. Weber, "Diskussion 1909," pp. 416–420.

This was Weber's position as of 1909. Obviously, it was at least partly tactical; it implied the possibility of scientific agreement among partisans of divergent value orientations, and it thus had little to do with the issues initially raised by Rickert.[10]

The Maxim and Ethos of Value Neutrality

The controversy over value judgments within the Social Policy Association reached a climax in 1914, when the association's steering committee *(Ausschuss)* held a closed meeting on the subject. To prepare for this meeting, Weber and others submitted memoranda that were printed in manuscript in 1913, and that addressed a whole cluster of interrelated questions, including the role of value judgments in classroom teaching. Weber's memorandum *(Gutachten)* on these issues is available to us, along with a revised and slightly expanded version of it that was published in 1917, and that referred to 'Value Neutrality' *(Wertfreiheit)* in its title. Finally, in late 1917, Weber delivered a lecture to a liberal student organization (a branch of the *Freie Studentenschaft*) that was transcribed and subsequently revised for publication in 1919 under the title "Science as a Vocation." Taken together, the memorandum of 1913, the revised essay of 1917, and the lecture of 1917/1919 provide a systematic account of Weber's passionately held views on the relationship between science and value judgments.[11]

At the most practical level, Weber objected to "prophecy" in the classroom; he sought to dissuade his academic colleagues from testifying to their value preferences from the lectern. Admitting that it might be difficult to keep one's scholarly work free of personal bias, he nevertheless insisted upon value neutrality as a regulative ideal of *Wissenschaft*. The possibility of ordinary error too, he noted, "proves nothing against the duty to search for truth." He particularly disliked the suggestion that, while the line between scholarship and value judgment is difficult to draw in practice, university teachers should at least avoid excessively "partisan" positions. The view that the class-

10. Ibid., esp. pp. 419–420.
11. On the 1917/1919 lecture, see *MWG* I/17, pp. 49–69.

room is no place for "passion" struck him as a "bureaucrat's opinion that every independent teacher would have to reject." The overt preaching of political creeds by such men as Heinrich von Treitschke seemed to him less dangerous to the students' autonomy than the covert suggestion of ideologies in nominally 'dispassionate' ways. He was not sanguine about prospects for the traditional academic ideal of forming whole persons and propagating integral *Weltanschauungen*. He suspected that the modern universities could be most useful precisely by purveying *specialized training,* along with the purely scholarly virtue of "intellectual rectitude." At the same time, far from wanting to turn all students into mere specialists, Weber wrote, he meant to leave them free to make their own ultimate "life decisions" without interference from their professors.[12]

Weber expressly criticized Schmoller, and particularly Schmoller's search for a broadly acceptable consensus on social policy objectives. As Weber reported, Schmoller used to insist that university lectures be exempted from press reports and public debate. But Weber could accept this "privilege" only with respect to specialized analyses in the professor's field of competence. Surely the academic should not exploit his institutionally protected authority to impose his so-ciopolitical commitments upon a dependent audience. Would-be prophets should not avoid the overt contest of views in the public arena. Characteristically, Schmoller once proposed to exclude 'Marxists' and 'Manchesterites' from university chairs, while a jurist drew the line at 'anarchists.' But if political orientations were to be discussed at the universities at all, Weber argued, then all possible standpoints had to be represented. It was admittedly hard to imagine heterodox views being expressed in an academic system that still excluded criticism of the monarchy. Yet in principle, as Weber wrote, an anarchist might be a good student of the law.

> And if he is, then his . . . standpoint outside the conventions and presuppositions we take for granted . . . will enable him to discern problematic aspects in the foundations of the usual legal

12. Weber, "Wertfreiheit," pp. 489–491; "Gutachten," pp. 103–105; "Wissen-schaft," pp. 95–98.

doctrines that elude all those for whom they are too self-evi-dent. For the most radical doubt is the father of insight.

Weber thus sharply repudiated the view that "the path to scientific 'objectivity' may be entered by weighing the divergent value positions and [reaching] a 'statesmanlike' compromise."[13]

Extending his argument against value commitments based upon consensus, Weber also opposed the notion that ethical or social norms may be deduced from the direction of historical development. He was thinking not of Emile Durkheim's historical functionalism, but of German historical economists who took their 'ethical' orientation to be consistent with the actual evolution of capitalism. In response, Weber granted that particular policies must be chosen in the light of changing circumstances; but he would not admit that policy *objectives* should be altered to accommodate historical trends.

> Human beings are sufficiently inclined . . . to adjust to . . . the promise of success, not only in the means by which they seek to realize their . . . ideals, but by abandoning these ideals themselves. . . . It is hard to see why . . . the representatives of an empirical discipline should feel the need to support [this inclination]. . . . [Politics may be] the art of the possible. But . . . the possible has often been attained only because people aimed beyond it, for the impossible. It has not, after all, been the . . . ethics of 'adjustment' . . . the bureaucrat's morality of Confucianism, that has created the . . . positive . . . qualities of our culture.

A revolutionary syndicalist, Weber suggested, might act from pure conviction, rather than in the light of immediate prospects. Here again, Weber was mainly concerned with the human and cultural threat of a homogenizing conformism.[14]

13. Weber, "Wertfreiheit," pp. 492–499, esp. pp. 496, 499; "Gutachten," pp. 109–112.
14. Weber, "Wertfreiheit," pp. 512–517, esp. pp. 513–514; "Gutachten," pp. 122–127.

The conceptual core of Weber's case for value neutrality, however, was the logical distinction between theoretical and practical reasoning, descriptive and prescriptive propositions, *is* and *ought*. Weber's insistence upon this divide may have been inspired by his youthful enthusiasm for the work of Friedrich Albert Lange; but his explicit references were to Immanuel Kant. He argued that the 'formal' principles of Kant's practical philosophy did have 'material' or substantive implications in particular situations; but he did not believe that the guidance they provided was sufficiently specific in all cases. In the tradition of the German theory of *Bildung,* moreover, he thought it possible to imagine human values that transcended the framework of Kantian ethics. He rejected the suggestion that value commitments were merely 'subjective,' a matter of taste. Still, he believed that individuals could be deeply committed to radically divergent cultural values, from the aesthetic to the erotic. Accordingly, value judgments could and should be intensely debated, preferably in the public forum; but they should not be confounded with empirical and causal questions.[15]

Against Schmoller, Weber thus argued that empirical investigations cannot possibly provide valid norms.

> The validity of a practical imperative as a norm and . . . the truth value of an empirical proposition lie on absolutely heterogeneous problem levels. . . . The empirical-psychological and historical investigation of a certain value standpoint in its individual, social, and historical conditioning can never lead to anything other than its interpretive explanation.

To understand the value judgments of others is of course crucial for fruitful debates about normative questions—and about the ultimate objectives of social policies. Still, at least in principle, Weber saw value orientations as individual choices, which is why he adopted John Stuart Mill's image of "polytheism" in the moral realm.

15. The link to Lange is suggested in an unpublished paper by Bjarne Jacobsen, who is continuing to explore this question. For the rest, see the following note.

> The . . . unavoidable fruit from the tree of knowledge is none
> other than this: to . . . [see] the contradictions [among possible
> normative orientations], and thus to . . . recognize that every
> important action and . . . life as a whole, if it is consciously lived
> . . . [involves] ultimate decisions, through which the soul . . .
> chooses . . . its own fate.

The image of the 'soul choosing its fate' through 'ultimate decisions' may be disturbing, and we need to come back to it. But we
should recognize even now that it served as an antithesis to the
vision of a consensually or historically grounded policy science, as
well as to other problematic aspects of Weber's intellectual environment.[16]

Thus, coming back to the Social Policy Association, Weber remarked that its reformism used to reflect an ordinary sense of justice;
but this was no longer the case. Instead, the dissemination of values
from the lectern had become a "subjective" need and a "right of the
personality." It was this officially protected *personal* "prophecy" that
Weber could not bear. It was bound to have a disastrous effect upon
young people, who needed to focus upon specific tasks, to face
possibly unpleasant facts, and to "subordinate their own personality
to the matter or cause at hand" *(die Sache)*.

> It just isn't true . . . that 'the personality' . . . must be lost, so
> to speak, if it does not come into view on every occasion. . . .
> There is only one way to become [a personality, and that is] the
> unreserved commitment to a task or cause.

Weber was clearly concerned *as an educator* about certain currents
in his culture. He urgently reminded "professional thinkers" of their
obligation to "keep a cool head" and the capacity to "swim against
the tide." In his 1917 article, he moved directly from this injunction
to an attack upon the rhetoric of the 'cultural war.' "The German
ideas of 1914," he wrote, "were a literati's product," and the

---

16. Weber, "Wertfreiheit," pp. 501–508, esp. pp. 501, 503, 507–508; "Gutachten," pp. 114–118.

so-called socialism of the future is a rhetorical cover for further bureaucratization combined with corporate control. The ideological sanctification of such projects in terms of German philosophical idealism is a "repulsive breach of taste by self-important literati"—most of whom were Weber's academic colleagues.[17]

In 1917 and more fully in 1919, Weber also discussed another contemporary "fashion," the quest for intuitive insight and "vital experience" *(Erleben)*. Not only in research but in business and other fields, he observed, innovation typically requires some sort of "inspiration." This usually follows upon persistent analytical work, but it cannot be counted on even then. The inspiration of a dilettante may be potentially as fruitful as that of an expert, except that only the expert can test and develop it. In any case, Weber suspected that anxieties about the need for inspiration helped to sustain a widespread obsession with "vital experience," an "idol" as celebrated as that of "personality." The passion for *Erleben*, especially among students, presumably grew out of certain interpretations of Wilhelm Dilthey, who stressed the initially unstructured and integral character of pretheoretical, 'lived' experience. In plain German, Weber commented, this phenomenon used to be called "sensation." Yet nowadays, people try to prove themselves "personalities," rather than mere specialists, by means of a 'vital experience.' Worse, young people yearn not only for 'life' and *Erleben* but also for teachers who are personal "leaders," not just experts. They fail to realize that very few professors have leadership qualities, and almost never those who claim they do.[18]

While trying to restrain the yen for value judgments in learning and teaching, Weber moved toward a critique of his culture that became ever more comprehensive between 1914 and 1919. One of the issues he thus took up was the problem of 'progress.' He acknowledged that improved 'technical' solutions could permit genuine advances in a variety of fields, including architecture and music. He also accepted Georg Simmel's argument that a long-term

---

17. Weber, "Wertfeiheit," pp. 491–494, esp. p. 494; see also p. 540; "Gutachten," pp. 105–108.

18. Weber, "Wertfreiheit," p. 519; "Wissenschaft," pp. 81–84, 101–103.

"process" of social and individual "differentiation" was tending to diversify human orientations. But he warned against the tacit equation of this "process" with "progress" toward an increase in the "inner wealth" of human beings. Similarly, an advance of "rationalization" could certainly be observed in modern Western societies. Yet ("subjective") rationalization as such did not necessarily entail "progress" toward "right rationality," even in the purely technical sense. That is why economic policies could not be evaluated in terms of purely 'scientific' standards of productivity. For policy choices are unambiguous only when the purposes are given and the class structure assumed to be constant as well, so that only the economic means are at issue. More important, the need for extra-scientific value judgments would persist even if all technical questions were fully resolved.

> For . . . behind the 'action' stands: the human being . . . [for whom] the increase in the subjective rationality and in the objective-technical 'rightness' of the action . . . may mean a threat to important . . . values.

To understand Weber's defense of value neutrality, one has to have a sense of the positions he *opposed*.[19]

In his lecture of 1917/1919, Weber identified all of specialized "science" *(Wissenschaft)* with "progress." While describing specialization as an absolute precondition of scientific innovation, he also insisted that "science" extends beyond technical skills, to encompass knowledge for its own sake. Indeed, he identified *Wissenschaft* as "the most important segment" of the "process of intellectualization" that has been under way for "thousands of years," and that "nowadays provokes such negative reactions." He noted that this "rationalization" does not produce "increased general knowledge" about our "conditions of existence." Rather, it conveys the conviction that we could *find out* about these conditions, that *in principle,* "there are no mysterious incalculable powers. . . . [And] that

---

19. Weber, "Wertfreiheit," pp. 518–519, 525–530, esp. pp. 529–530; "Gutachten," pp. 127–134.

means: the disenchantment of the world." Unlike our ancestors, as Tolstoy pointed out, we can never know more than a fraction of our culture, which makes our individual deaths incongruous. In Plato's day, the philosopher could find the way from the shadows of appearance to the light of "true being"; in the Renaissance, empirical knowledge could lead to "true nature" and "true art"; in the seventeenth century, a naturalist could find "proof of God's wisdom in the anatomy of a louse." But nowadays no one believes that science can "teach us anything about the meaning of the world." If anything, it tends to "eradicate the belief" that there is such a "meaning." And of course Nietzsche has cured us of the faith that technological advance will lead to general "happiness." So perhaps Tolstoy rightly insisted that science is pointless, since it does not answer our most important question: "What should we do? How should we live?"[20]

As Weber indicated both in his 1917 essay and in his lecture of 1917/1919, he did *not* mean to exclude systematic discussion of value questions. He not only argued that empirically grounded causal knowledge should affect the assessment of proposed policies—and of their probable side effects; he also urged the analysis of ultimate "value axioms" for their logical coherence and their more or less consistent consequences. Briefly referring to the problems raised by Rickert, he observed that every type of scientific inquiry must presuppose that its findings are of interest. Thus the natural sciences can only assume that we *want* to know the laws of the universe, while the cultural and social sciences presuppose judgments of "value relatedness" that guide the selection of topics for study. Here again, however, Weber meant to replace tacit presuppositions with self-conscious "value analysis." He believed that the practitioners of *Wissenschaft* could foster explicit and coherent value commitments.

[As logicians], we can tell you that this or that practical position can be consistently . . . deduced . . . from this or that fundamental world view. . . . For you necessarily arrive at these or those . . . meaningful consequences if you remain true to

20. Weber, "Wissenschaft," pp. 80–81, 85–93, esp. pp. 86–87, 92–93.

yourselves. . . . Thus . . . we can oblige or at least aid the individual to give himself an account of his actions. This does not seem to me a small matter. . . . I am tempted to say . . . of a teacher who succeeds in this that he serves 'ethical' objectives: the duty to foster clarity and . . . responsibility.

A moral action, for Weber, was performed after a full analysis of its probable consequences and grounded in a deliberate and internally consistent value orientation.[21]

At the same time, Weber strenuously insisted upon the diversity of ultimate value choices—and upon the irreconcilable conflict among them. Referring to Friedrich Nietzsche und to Charles Baudelaire, he argued that "something may be holy . . . *although* . . . [and even] *in so far as* it is not beautiful," and beautiful though evil, and "true . . . though not beautiful and not holy and not good." Surely no one would think of scientifically "refuting" the "ethic of the Sermon on the Mount," and yet one could certainly opt instead for the injunction to "resist evil," lest one "share responsibility for its overwhelming power." In the post-Christian era, with "the old gods rising from their graves," we must face our inability scientifically to resolve "the contest among the ultimate possible orientations toward life, and thus the necessity of [personally] deciding among them." That is the sense in which Weber repeatedly evoked the image of "polytheism."[22]

In the concluding pages of his lecture of 1917/1919, Weber brought together his cultural analysis and his case against academic prophecy.

That science today is a specialized 'profession' . . . [which seeks] self-consciousness and knowledge of factual interrelationships . . . [rather than] spiritual goods and revelations dispensed by . . . seers . . . or . . . wise men . . . about the *meaning* of the world . . . is an inescapable given of our historical situation.

---

21. Weber, "Wertfreiheit," pp. 510–512; "Gutachten," pp. 119–122; "Wissenschaft," pp. 93–95, and esp. pp. 103–104.

22. Ibid., pp. 99–101, 104–105; italics mine.

If in line with Tolstoy's question, we yearn for a savior, Weber continued, we have to recognize that he *"just isn't there."* It will not help to have "thousands of professors trying to take over his role as little prophets salaried and privileged by the state." Religions rest upon presuppositions that are exempt from scientific inquiry. They demand the "sacrifice of the intellect," opening an "unbridgeable gulf between [themselves] and science." In any case, no genuine prophecy has ever emerged from "the need of some intellectuals" to "furnish their souls" with a decorative spirituality, or with "surrogate" forms of "vital experience" that are suitable for the "book market": "All that is simply: fraud and self-deception."23

The search of many young people for communal relationships, while more serious, is probably not enhanced by being interpreted in a religious sense.

> It is the fate of our time, with its . . . rationalization and . . . above all: the disenchantment of the world, that precisely the . . . most sublime values have retreated from the public sphere, either into the . . . realm of mystical life or into the brotherliness of immediate personal relationships. It is no accident that our highest art is intimate and not monumental. . . . If we try to . . . 'invent' monumental [art], the results are [the] lamentable miscreations of the last twenty years. . . . [It is the same with] new religious forms without a . . . genuine prophecy.

Those who "cannot manfully bear the fate of the times" should quietly return to the "arms of the old churches," offering the "sacrifice of the intellect"; for that is at least honest. But our true obligation is to "intellectual rectitude." Instead of feigning a new prophecy, or yearning for it, we must "do justice to the demands of the day," which requires each of us to "find and obey the demon who holds the threads of his life."24

23. Ibid., pp. 105–109, esp. pp. 105, 108–109.
24. Ibid, pp. 109–111.

Some of Weber's formulations seem deliberately extravagant. The image of a 'demon' directing the individual's 'fate' is a case in point, since nothing that Weber wrote about value commitments evokes anything like the passivity implied by the metaphor. In the same way, Weber's rhetoric sometimes makes the personal 'decision' in favor of an ultimate value standpoint appear more radically gratuitous than any relevant choices he actually describes. After all, agents who choose their lines of action after fully reflecting upon the coherence and consistency of their ultimate objectives—and after thinking through the probable consequences and side effects of what they propose to do—can hardly be said to act in a spirit of untutored voluntarism, especially if they at least initially consider Kantian universalist principles as well.

But as Wilhelm Hennis has suggested, there is a way to account for Weber's tendency to overstate certain aspects of his position, which has to do with his *pedagogical* concerns. Following H. H. Bruun and others, one has to recognize that Weber was quite as anxious to safeguard the autonomy of the student's value choices against certain forms of scientism and conformism as he was to protect *Wissenschaft* from the intrusion of personal value preferences. *As an educator and as a moralist,* he meant to foster the capacity for independent commitment to a 'cause' as well as minds capable of intellectual clarity and tough-minded realism. Rightly or wrongly, he interpreted Schmoller's brand of social policy, along with certain attitudes among his contemporaries, as profound threats, not only to science and reason but also to the human personality and the vitality of his culture.[25]

In any case, it should now be clear beyond any question that Weber's arguments for value neutrality in social science and social policy owe almost nothing to the considerations initially raised by Rickert. Certainly, Weber was in no sense a 'subjectivist' or a 'relativist.' On the contrary, his position anticipated that of current spokesmen for interpretation on the principle of 'rationality,' who are also generally hostile to relativism.

25. See Bruun, *Science, Values, and Politics;* Käsler, *Einführung;* and esp. Hennis, "Volle Nüchternheit."

Contemporary Formulations

In the contemporary Anglo-American world as among Weber's contemporaries, a number of theoreticians have seen an irreconcilable difference between interpretation and explanation. Until fairly recently, in fact, some philosophers have claimed that actions do not have 'causes' at all. Their main argument has been that actions are internally or logically related to the *intentions* embodied in them, *whereas causes must be separate from their effects and contingently related to them.* But Alasdair MacIntyre and Donald Davidson have challenged this position, though on somewhat different grounds.

MacIntyre has called attention to an agent's being *given a reason* or *afforded a motive* to perform a certain action. The event in which this happens, according to MacIntyre, can be a cause of the ensuing action, provided that the 'cause' is understood as a necessary condition (not a sufficient one), or as 'a lever,' something that intervened (in Weber's sense) to *bring about* the action it explains.

> I may discover that when you are in a certain frame of mind I can get you to act by giving you information which affords a motive or a reason. Your action bears testimony to the fact that it was this motive or reason on which you were acting (as returning a ring with a reproachful letter is testimony that the girl's motive arises from her information about the man's behavior).

Here the affording of the motive is not a sufficient condition for the action, and "we do not depend on a universal generalization of whose truth we need to be assured in order to make the connection."

> Even if another occasion affording the same kind of motive does not produce the same action, we should not have cause for doubting what caused the girl to act as she did on the first occasion.

MacIntyre does *not* mean to say that actions never have causes that are sufficient conditions. Thus drugs may affect human actions (and not only bodily movements); or I may find that I regularly become angry within five minutes of beginning to lose at cards. Nevertheless, the causes of actions are often less than sufficient conditions; instead, they play the role of an ice patch on a road that brings about an accident in a particular case.[26]

Davidson offers a more radical challenge to the view that actions do not have causes, but are defined by the intentions they embody. The *rationalization* that links an action to its agent's reason for acting, he argues, is a species of causal explanation after all. The agent's reason is a conjunction of a "pro-attitude" and a belief. Pro-attitudes may be "desires, wantings, urges, promptings, and a great variety of moral views, aesthetic principles, economic prejudices, social conventions, and public and private goals and values." Agents have pro-attitudes toward actions of certain kinds, and they believe that the actions they perform are of those kinds. Taken together, their pro-attitudes and the associated beliefs are their *reasons* for acting, and these reasons are also the *causes* of the actions. They are certainly logically distinct from the actions they rationalize. (The action of turning on the light can be redescribed as an event in which the light is turned on in a particular way; but this is not true of the *intention* to turn on the light.) "Central to the relation between a reason and an action it explains," Davidson adds, "is the idea that the agent performed the action *because* he had the reason." This tends to undermine the view that in an essentially interpretive context, historians simply elucidate the actions they consider by pointing to rational consideration upon which they *might* have been based.[27]

Davidson subscribes to the covering law model of explanation in its deductive nomological version, although he modifies it in crucial respects:

> The laws whose existence is required if reasons are causes of action, do not, we may be sure, deal in the concepts in which rationalizations must deal. If the causes of a class of events

---

26. MacIntyre, "Antecedents of Action," pp. 204, 206–207, esp. p. 206.
27. Davidson, "Actions, Reasons, and Causes," pp. 3–6, 9.

(actions) fall in a certain class (reasons) and there is a law to back each singular causal statement, it does not follow that there is any law connecting events classified as reasons with events classified as actions—the classifications may even be neurological, chemical, or physical.[28]

Thus successful causal claims may be 'covered' by 'laws' that are not (yet) known, and that are not phrased in terms similar to those used in the singular causal explanations they sustain. Davidson's concluding reference to classifications that "may even be neurological, chemical, or physical" could be meant to suggest that explanations of actions will ultimately be found to rest upon the laws of 'neurology, chemistry, or physics.' If that is Davidson's thought, then Weber would have disagreed with him. Yet Weber certainly *could* have accepted the broader claim that the causes of actions may be the agents' reasons for acting, a claim quite independent of Davidson's extra-empirical hint about the possible role of psychophysical laws.

In 1958 Peter Winch published a little book that has since received a good deal of attention as a challenge to "the idea of a social science." Winch's position draws upon aspects of Ludwig Wittgenstein's philosophy; it also faintly recalls the claims of Rudolf Stammler, which Weber so strenuously opposed. For Winch, languages and the 'forms of life' that sustain them are necessarily 'rule-governed,' and this raises problems for those disposed to search for 'regularities' in social life.

> To investigate the type of regularity studied in a given kind of inquiry is to examine the nature of the rule according to which judgments of identity are made in that enquiry. Such judgments are intelligible only relatively to a given mode of human behavior, governed by its own rules. . . . The concepts and criteria according to which the sociologist judges that, in two situations, the same thing has happened, or the same action performed, must be understood *in relation to the rules governing sociological*

28. Ibid., p. 17.

investigation. But . . . whereas in the case of the natural scientist we have to deal with only one set of rules, namely those governing the scientist's investigation . . . *what the sociologist is studying,* as well as his study of it, is a human activity . . . carried on according to rules. And it is these rules, rather than those which govern the sociologist's investigation, which specify what is to count as 'doing the same kind of thing' in relation to that kind of activity. . . . Although the reflective student of society . . . may find it necessary to use concepts which are not taken from the forms of activity which he is investigating, but . . . from the context of his own investigation, still these technical concepts of his will imply previous understanding of those other concepts which belong to the activities under investigation.

In effect, Winch restates the old thesis that actions must be interpreted 'in their own terms,' and can never be 'explained' in terms of discoverable 'regularities.' At a minimum, his arguments forbid accounts of actions that depart too far from the self-understanding of the agents involved; followed to their most radical implications, they exclude the analysis of cultures by anyone not already steeped in the 'rules' that 'govern' them.[29]

In response to Winch, MacIntyre begins with a modest restatement of Winch's interpretationist proposal.

An action is *first* made intelligible as the outcome of motives, reasons, and decisions; and it is then made *further* intelligible by those motives, reasons, and decisions being set in the context of the rules of a given form of social life.

But MacIntyre then proceeds to his criticisms.

A distinction may be made between those rules which agents in a given society sincerely profess to follow . . . and those . . . which . . . do in fact guide their acts. . . . The making of this distinction is essential to the notions of *ideology* and of *false*

29. Winch, *Idea of a Social Science,* esp. pp. 83–84, 86–87, 89.

consciousness, notions which are extremely important to some non-Marxist as well as to Marxist social scientists.

More generally, Winch uses the concept of a rule so loosely "that quite different senses of *rule-governed* are . . . confounded. . . . If I go for a walk . . . are my actions rule-governed in the sense in which my . . . playing chess [is] rule-governed?"

In societies like ours, occupational and social "roles" provide norms of action; but the norms that define the role of the headwaiter, for example, do not "constrain the individual." In an asylum, by contrast, "the behavior of patients is determined to a considerable degree by institutional arrangements which provide a severely limited set of possible roles." The scheme offered by Winch is flawed because it does not allow us to distinguish between rules that do, and rules that do not, function as causally relevant restraints upon the individual. In short:

> We can in a given society discover a variety of systematic regularities. There are the systems of rules which agents professedly follow; there are the systems of rules which they actually follow; there are causal regularities exhibited in the correlation of statuses and forms of behavior, and of one form of behavior and another, which are not rule-governed at all; there are regularities which are in themselves neither causal nor rule-governed, although dependent for their existence perhaps on regularities of both types, such as cyclical patterns of development exhibited in some societies; and there are interrelationships which exist between all these. Winch concentrates on some of these at the expense of others.

This comes remarkably close to what Weber said about Stammler.[30]

Since about 1980, a theory of 'rational' interpretation has emerged that seems even more thoroughly consistent with Weber's methodology than MacIntyre's comments upon social 'rules.' The new theory can be read as a rejoinder not only to Winch, but also

---

30. MacIntyre, "Idea of a Social Science," esp. pp. 115, 118–120, 122, for this and what preceded.

to a 'strong' relativist program put forward by Barry Barnes and David Bloor. Steven Lukes, a leading spokesman and historian of the new theory, puts the case against relativism as follows.

> In the very identification of beliefs and *afortiori* of belief systems we must presuppose commonly shared standards of truth and inference. . . . Neither the evidence of cross-cultural variation in schemes of classification, nor that of radically divergent theoretical schemes or styles of reasoning, nor arguments for the possible applicability of alternative logics undermine this position, which must, indeed, be accepted before the problem of relativism can be set up in the first place. . . . Only from a bridgehead of common beliefs can the uncommon be discerned.

In further elaboration of this view, Lukes cites Davidson on the interpretive "Principle of Charity."

> The basic strategy must be to assume that by and large a speaker we do not yet understand is consistent and correct in his beliefs—according to our standards, of course. Following this strategy makes it possible to pair up sentences the speaker utters with sentences of our own that we hold true under like circumstances. When this is done systematically, the result is a method of translation. Once the project is under way, it is possible, and indeed necessary, to allow for some slack for error or differences of opinion. But we cannot make sense of error until we have established a base of agreement.

Obviously, this formulation is largely identical with Weber's account of interpretation on the initial assumption of 'right rationality.' Weber wrote about the interpretation of actions, rather than beliefs; but since Davidson's 'reasons for acting' are conjunctions of 'pro-attitudes' and 'beliefs,' his subject matter is really equivalent to Weber's.[31]

---

31. In addition to Wilson, ed., *Rationality,* see Hollis and Lukes, eds., *Rationality and Relativism,* esp. Lukes, "Relativism in Its Place," pp. 262–263.

Lukes is not quite satisfied with the Principle of Charity, however, since "it bases the necessary agreement" with those we interpret "on too many truths."

> Some truths we hold to may be ones they could not intelligibly have acquired, and it may be far easier to explain their disagreeing with us. As Richard Grandy has put it . . . it may be better to attribute to them an explicable falsehood than a mysterious truth. Instead of the Principle of Charity, Grandy proposes the Principle of Humanity . . . 'the condition that the imputed pattern of relations among beliefs, desires and the world be as similar to our own as possible.' . . . On this principle, what must be presupposed before translation can begin involves both rationality and explicability. Judgments as to rationality will affect our judgments as to explicability. If [the beliefs at issue] are true and rationally held, they will be explicable; if they are false, their being held must be explicable, but a different kind of explanation may be needed depending on whether they are rationally or irrationally held. . . . The Principle of Charity counselled 'Count them right in most matters.' The Principle of Humanity counsels 'Count them intelligible, or perhaps count them right unless we can't explain their being right or can better explain their being wrong.'

This is fascinating, not only because it closely parallels Weber's distinction between 'right rationality' and 'subjective rationality,' but above all because it demonstrates the inevitability of the link so strongly urged by Weber between interpretation and explanation. For Lukes and Grandy as for Weber, there *must be* a single analytical framework in which the investigator can move from the rational interpretation to the (causal) explanation of beliefs. Interpretation and explanation, as Weber recognized, are simultaneous and interactive approaches to the actions and texts of the past.[32]

Much of what has been said about contemporary views of interpretation can in fact be restated in the terminology of reasons and

32. Lukes, "Relativism in Its Place," p. 264.

causes. The antecedents of actions and beliefs may be reasons, including good reasons; but they may also be causes other than reasons. To undertake the necessary discriminations in particular cases, we are best served by the single overall scheme of a reason or other cause as something that intervenes in a process, and that alters the outcome to be expected in its absence. We *must* be able to ask whether it was a possible reason and/or something else that 'made a difference' in the outward course of behaviors or pattern of belief we want to understand. Indeed, it strikes me that this question plays a role in our moral life as well. Before considering whether our reasons for acting are ethically acceptable, after all, we must know whether it is our reasons, or causes other than our reasons, that shape our behaviors. We want our actions to be fully explicable in terms of our best reasons; but we should be on the lookout for cases in which they are predictable *apart from* our reasons. Here again, we must be able to weigh reasons in the same analytical balance with other possible antecedents of action and belief.

For the historian, good reasons are the usual causes of valid beliefs and right actions. Typically, the beliefs involved are fully reflected and rationally held. Yet some actions are ill advised, and some beliefs are either false, or neither true nor false. They are irrationally held, and they call for explanation in terms of causes other than good reasons. They might be traced to habit, to tacit custom, or to hallowed tradition. Or they might be perpetuated in incompletely conscious forms by prevailing institutional arrangements, patterns of practice, or social relations. Weber would have wanted to add that systems of belief are *not* mere effects of more fundamental historical forces. But that is an issue best deferred to the next chapter, which deals with the relationship between Weber's methodological principles and his actual work as a practitioner of the cultural and social sciences.

FROM THEORY TO PRACTICE

6

It is obviously impossible to discuss Weber's substantive works in a few pages. To understand many of his specific analyses fully, in any case, one has to study them in conjunction with his political views, and his comparative historical sociology of religion calls for an even broader interpretive context. No concerted approach to these topics can here be attempted. Yet it seems important to look at least briefly at the relationship between Weber's methodology and his practice as a cultural and social scientist. In portions of what follows, I will discuss selected theoretical texts with obvious practical implications; in other passages, I will draw upon preliminary impressions of some of Weber's substantive theses. This is not a very satisfactory approach; but it is surely preferable to a discussion of Weber's methodology that takes no account at all of his practice.

Neither Marxism nor Idealism

As Karl Löwith observed long ago, Weber repeatedly criticized a form of 'Marxism' that had less to do with the writings of Karl Marx—not to mention the early Marx—than it did with certain orthodoxies of the late nineteenth century: with dogmatic historical 'materialism' and economic determinism. *At some level,* Weber's account of the human condition in modern society has much in common with what Marx wrote about 'alienation.' Quite apart from his somber analysis of rationalization and bureaucratization, moreover, Weber contrasted the 'formal' or 'instrumental' rationality of capitalism with its 'substantive' irrationality, its radical inadequacy from a variety of human perspectives. In this and other respects, he took Marx very seriously. At the same time, he flatly rejected the notion that all causal connections in history can 'ultimately' be traced back to economic conditions, however defined, or that all historical processes are essentially unidirectional. While this is generally recognized, it should not be overinterpreted to mean that Weber championed the primacy of 'spiritual' forces, historical 'idealism,' or the creative role of 'great men' in history. Thus, as Löwith has pointed out, Weber's 'spirit of capitalism' is *neither deducible* from, *nor* is it the *sole cause* of, modern capitalism. And even his 'charismatic' leaders owe their 'gifts' at least partly to the crises that bring them to the fore—and to the perceptions of their followers.[1]

Weber's sharpest attack upon 'historical materialism' came in his 1907 critique of Rudolf Stammler, which is ironic in itself, for Stammler had stressed the constitutive significance of legal norms and social 'rules' as a way of 'overcoming' doctrinaire Marxism. Apparently, he feared that without recourse to 'rules,' a consistently causal approach to social life would ultimately have to rest upon physical laws about the constituent 'elements' of reality. "This flawed and scientifically useless analogy," Weber wrote, is still alive in "the heads of some historical materialists." Stammler's vague remarks about "the law of causation," Weber thought, implied "the causal 'world formula' that some adherents of naturalism dream about." He further objected to the tacit equation of Marxist "historical materialism" with a genuinely "materialist" ontology, although there is of course no relationship between these two species of "materialism."[2]

At a 1910 meeting of the Social Policy Association, Weber put his case against a monocausal economism a little more bluntly.

I just . . . want to register a protest against . . . the proposition expressed here that anything, be it technology or be it econom-

---

1. Löwith, *Weber and Marx,* pp. 18–67, and esp. 100–107.
2. Weber, "Stammler," pp. 316–318.

ics, is the . . . 'ultimate' or 'essential' cause of anything else. If we consider the chain of causation, [we will find that] it runs sometimes from technological to economic and political, sometimes from political to religious and then to economic matters, etc. At no point do we come to a resting place.

As a matter of fact, Weber did not think much of the conventional subdivision of the cultural and social world. Yet he was a legitimate heir of the German historical school of economics in at least one important respect. He believed that the "science of economics" should deal not only with the economic "codetermination of all social phenomena," but also with "the conditioning of economic processes and economic systems" by noneconomic phenomena, prominently including "political actions and formations . . . above all: the state and the laws guaranteed by the state." Here is a case in which Weber continued a methodological preference embodied in his scholarly tradition. He not only favored a *multicausal* approach to the cultural and social world; he also saw the historical 'chain of causation' running in *divergent* and occasionally *opposed* directions, depending upon the circumstances.[3]

In his 1915 Introduction to his comparative sociology of religion, Weber dealt somewhat more fully with the relationship between social stratification and religious belief. He argued that the major world religions were associated in characteristic ways with social strata that functioned as their predominant 'carriers,' though not their only ones. Confucianism, for example, was linked to the status ethic of an office-holding literary elite; Buddhism was perpetuated by mendicant monks; Islam was a warrior religion; while Christianity initially attracted a following among wandering artisans, and essentially remained a specifically urban and 'burgher' religion. Yet Weber cautioned against a one-sided view of these connections.

It is in no way the thesis of the following exposition that the distinctive character of a religion is merely a function of the social position of the stratum that seems its characteristic carrier

3. Weber, "Diskussion 1910," p. 456; "Wertfreiheit," p. 538.

. . . its 'ideology,' or a 'reflection' of its material or ideal interests.

The reference to 'ideal interests' is highly significant in itself. It acknowledges the unmistakable competition among occupational and social groups, not only about economic, legal, and political advantages but also about status issues, role definitions, and other forms of symbolic power. Much of what is distinctive about Weber's analytical *practice* grew out of his insistence upon an enlarged conception of social 'interests.' Yet even in the context of this expanded conception, Weber could not accept the mere deduction of the religious from the social. For once a religion is formed, as he noted, it usually influences the way of life of "quite heterogeneous strata." Consistent with this position, Weber expressed serious reservations about Friedrich Nietzsche's overly general equation of Christianity with the "resentment" of the oppressed.[4]

Yet Weber did not mean to suggest anything like the primacy of 'ideas' or of spiritual forces in history. About this, too, he was quite explicit.

Material and ideal interests, not ideas, directly dominate the actions of human beings. But: the 'world views' created by 'ideas' have often served as switches, setting the tracks along which the dynamics of interest moved the actions forward.

This famous passage, I believe, should be read quite literally, in the light of Weber's model of singular causal analysis. For that model is ideally suited to display causal forces or activating tendencies, which are then guided into specific 'tracks' by means of 'switches.' In the case at hand, we are offered the image of interests launching a 'dynamic' that is channeled by religiously grounded world views. The phrasing suggests two steps, each of which involves one or more causes and processes; but there is a clear difference between the impetus provided by material and ideal interests, and the 'switch' that sets the specific course of change, the switch provided by

4. Weber, "Einleitung," pp. 83–97, esp. pp. 87–88.

"ideas." In a Weberian causal analysis, the focus would be upon the way in which a world view *brought about* a particular historical sequence and outcome, *rather than* possible alternatives. The formulation is even more exactly characteristic of Weber than has been commonly recognized.[5]

At least one other set of arguments in the Introduction of Weber's sociology of religion should be considered as well. Discussing the broad range of specific occupational and social situations represented within the historical stratum of 'burghers' or bourgeois *(Bürger)*, Weber commented upon the "elective affinities to certain types of religiosity" that characterize this stratum. He went on to specify a "tendency toward a *practical* rationalism in the conduct of life." Despite the recurrent possibility of passive traditionalism or contemplative mysticism, Weber argued, the Western burgher stratum has shown a special propensity toward an "*ethically* rational regulation of life," typically on the basis of an "emissary prophecy" of this-worldly asceticism: "Not union with God or contemplative surrender to God . . . but God-willed *action* with the feeling of being God's "instrument" could here become the preferred religious habitus." The emissary prophecy that converted the devout into "instruments" of God, according to Weber, was further characterized by an "elective affinity" for a "super-mundane, personal, angry, forgiving, loving, demanding, punishing creator God," rather than the typically impersonal God of contemplative religiosity and exemplary prophecy.[6]

Without trying to follow Weber's substantive claims in detail, we should take note of his suggestion that a given "habitus" may express itself *both* in a certain range of religious beliefs *and* in a set of practical orientations toward life. We may picture the "affinity" involved as an *interactive* causal relationship, in which two patterns of action and belief *reinforce* each other. But it would also be consistent to follow the French sociologist Pierre Bourdieu's account of a habitus as a pretheoretical propensity to reproduce certain forms of thought and practice. Bourdieu describes "the

5. Ibid., p. 101.
6. Ibid., pp. 106–108.

habitus" as a "structuring structure" that is perpetuated at a tacit level by inherited practices, institutions, and social relations, especially by education, and that actually *engenders* a range of more specific articulations. Bourdieu's theories on the subject are influenced by the works of Karl Mannheim and Erwin Panofsky, as well as by Weber. He explicitly considers "the habitus" as a *cause* of intellectual orientations, which makes his views seem all the more consistent with those of Weber. In any case, what Weber wrote about "elective affinities" and about the "habitus" has little left in common with the conventional questions about the 'primacy' of 'social,' 'political' or 'cultural' forces within the historical process as a whole.[7]

From Methodological Individualism to the Comparative Analysis of Structural Change

Stephen Kalberg has favorably compared Weber's practice as a comparative historical sociologist with both 'world systems theory' and the 'thick description' favored by the 'interpretive historical' school. Kalberg identifies Weber with a 'causal analytical' direction in sociology; but he adds that even the practitioners of that approach have much to learn from (1) Weber's ability to relate the role of human agency to that of persistent historical structures, and (2) Weber's attention to the causal relevance of traditions and values, as against purely economic factors.[8]

I quite agree with Kalberg's assessment; but it raises questions that urgently require further discussion: How did Weber manage to *bridge the gap* between his emphasis upon human agency and his analysis of persistent historical structures? How could he consistently defend a form of *methodological individualism,* and still launch a comparative historical sociology of the world religions that was virtually *universal* in scope? And even more generally, how could his model of singular causal analysis be applied not only to

7. For a brief sketch of Bourdieu's views on these matters, see Ringer, *Fields of Knowledge,* pp. 4–10.

8. Kalberg, *Max Weber's Comparative-Historical Sociology.*

such 'small' events as the Defenestration of Prague, but also to such 'large' developments as the rise of modern capitalism? One way to address these questions is to distinguish between *events* and *processes* on the one hand, and between *microscopic* and *macroscopic* levels of analysis on the other. The Defenestration of Prague, for example, could be identified as a micro-event, and the rise of modern capitalism as a macro-process. Weber himself was certainly interested in processes as well as events, and the distinctions involved seem both reasonable and workable.

The difficulty is that they are also incorrigibly imprecise and even superficial. For there is no clear divide between microscopic and macroscopic events *or* processes. When we identify smoking as a cause of cancer, to be sure, we can expect to discover more specific processes that account for the connection.[9] But we cannot know whether all of these processes will be *irreducibly* microscopic—or deterministic. And our cognitive situation is even more precarious with respect to the micro-processes that may or may not sustain the causal relationships between particular reasons and singular actions. Perhaps the conventional divide between 'the mind' and 'the body' will prove to be misconceived? At least in the cultural and social world, there *may be* no such thing as an *irreducibly* microscopic level of analysis. As both Simmel and Weber showed, a singular relationship does not and cannot be specified as a set of connections among the elementary constituents of two successive total states. Similarly, as Salmon points out, a 'process' may be at least as macroscopic as a shopping trip or as microscopic as an electron circling an atomic nucleus.

Thus even the Defenestration of Prague could be described as a process, or a cluster of processes, while the rise of modern capitalism could be considered an event—on a sufficiently extended time scale—especially if one asked why that 'event' occurred in Western Europe, rather than elsewhere. The *logic* of causal analysis, in sum, does not change with the *generality* of the historical *developments and outcomes* that are to be explained. If one fails to realize that, one

9. Two days after I wrote this sentence, a step in that direction was widely reported.

is bound to detect a problematic tension between Weber's methodology and his practice.

Those who see such a tension are of course particularly troubled by Weber's *methodological individualism*, his theoretical focus upon the actions and beliefs of individuals, rather than upon the collective states that interested Emile Durkheim. As Weber repeatedly remarked, this theoretical preference grew directly out of his commitment to the interpretive method. Single individuals and their actions are the 'atoms' of sociology, he argued, because (and to the extent that) they are the objects of interpretation. For other analytical purposes, human beings may be bundles of chemical and psychophysical processes; but as the performers of actions and holders of beliefs, they cannot be reduced below the level of the integral individual. Indeed, "for the same reason, the individual is also . . . the upper limit [of analysis], and the sole bearer of meaningful behavior." Jurists might find it helpful and even necessary to refer to states and other organizations *as if* they were individuals. Historians in the Romantic tradition might be disastrously misled by 'organic' theories of the state or of other collectivities. For the interpretive sociologist, however, social entities and structures are strictly interrelationships or patterns of individual actions. An "action," to recall Weber's definition, is linked to a "subjective meaning"; a "social action" is "oriented in its progression to the behavior of others," and sociology as a discipline "seeks interpretively to understand social action and thereby causally to explain it in its progression and in its effects."[10]

Still, Weber clearly transcended the ostensibly narrow limits laid down in these initial stipulations, and he did so partly by aggregating the actions to be interpreted.

> Understanding . . . signifies the interpretation of the meaning or complex of meanings (a) actually intended in a particular case, or (b) intended on the average and approximately, or (c) to be constructed . . . for the pure type (ideal type) of a

10. Weber, "Kategorien," pp. 439, 454, esp. p. 439; "Grundbegriffe," pp. 6–7, and esp. p. 1.

frequent phenomenon. The concepts and 'laws' posited by pure economic theory, for example, are such ideal-typical constructions.

In his practice, Weber actually made little use of average and approximate meanings. But the construction of ideal types certainly helped him to deal with the actions and beliefs of social *groups* and even of whole *cultures*. One of the functions of the ideal type was hypothetically to characterize *collective* actions as more or less rational responses to given situations, and thus causally to ascribe *aspects* of actual group behaviors to the circumstances and orientations 'covered' by the type. As we know, ideal-typical analysis could move through several stages, aiming at successively closer approximations to observed progressions or patterns of behavior, and at a *rank order* of the interpretive and causal relationships as more or less decisive for the empirical outcome at issue. Whatever else may be said about this procedure, it cannot be equated with 'methodological individualism' in any narrow or dogmatic sense of that term.[11]

Also of great consequence was Weber's definition of *social* action in terms of *expectations* about the actions of others. To emphasize his point of view, Weber repeatedly cited examples of human behaviors that were *not* social actions in his sense, either because they had no meaning at all or because they were not performed with a view to the actions of others. Two bicyclists colliding in a purely physical accident, for example, are not engaged in meaningful social action, and neither are a plurality of persons who more or less simultaneously open their umbrellas at the onset of rain. Neither the 'mass psychology' of Gustave LeBon nor Gabriel Tarde's 'imitation' met Weber's definition of "social action," which *must be* "oriented toward the past, present, or expected future behavior of others."[12]

From 'social actions,' Weber moved naturally and easily to 'social relationships,' 'social structures,' and 'social orders.' A "social relationship," in Weber's definition, consists of "behaviors of several persons that are adjusted and oriented in their meanings to their

11. Weber, "Grundbegriffe," p. 4.
12. Ibid., p. 11; "Kategorien," pp. 454–455.

mutual interdependence." Social relationships may be as open and transitory as an economic exchange; or they may be relatively closed and enduring "formations" *(Gebilde),* as in the case of an artisanal guild or a political state. Social actions—and especially social relationships—may be affected by the agents' belief in "the existence of a legitimate order." The "validity" of an order for the participants may be based upon "tradition," "faith" in "the newly revealed or exemplary," "value rational" commitment, or belief in the "legality" of "positive statutes."[13]

For the sociologist, however, an order is empirically "valid" strictly by virtue of the *probability* or "chance" that it will affect the *actions of the participants.* Indeed, much the same is true of "social relationships" in general.

> The social relationship consists . . . exclusively of the chance that actions specifically oriented to each other in their meanings have taken place, even when [the relationships] are such . . . 'social formations' as a 'state.' . . . [Thus] a 'state' . . . ceases to exist sociologically as soon as the chance has faded that certain kinds of meaningfully oriented social actions will take place.

The recourse to probabilities is of course highly characteristic of Weber. In the cases of social "relationships" and legitimate "orders," the tactics of definition are clearly designed to replace "organic" or "emanationist" conceptions of social institutions and collectivities. Weber's stance could be loosely described as 'nominalist,' if only in this respect. In any case, Weber's line of analysis does allow him to move from methodological individualism to the study of complex social interactions and organizations. After all, he can stipulate that a state "exists" or "has ceased to exist," and that seems decisive.[14]

One also has to remember that Weber's theory of action extends well beyond the realm of deliberate and reflected agency. Like action

13. Weber, "Kategorien," pp. 443–444; "Grundbegriffe," pp. 13, 16, 17, 19, including for what follows.
14. Weber, "Grundbegriffe," p. 13, for block quotation.

generally, Weber held, social action may be "purposively rational," "value rational" (motivated by "conscious belief in the . . . value of a certain behavior . . . independently of its success"), "emotional," or "traditional," sustained by accustomed usage. Weber distinguished among merely habitual "usage" *(Brauch)*, enduring "custom" *(Sitte)*, informally sanctioned "convention," and formal "law." As in his roster of interpretive hypotheses, however, he took the alternatives to be linked by gradual transitions. In any case, the *rational action of the individual,* while methodologically significant as a point of departure, was never more than a *limiting case* in his overall scheme.[15]

Indeed, Weber repeatedly called attention to actions performed in a less than fully conscious way. "In the vast majority of cases," he wrote, "action takes place in dull semiconsciousness or unconsciousness." Only occasionally do some individuals raise the meanings of their actions to full consciousness. It is therefore often the sociologists, rather than the agents they seek to understand, who conceptualize behaviors by classifying them in terms of "possibly intended meanings."[16] As Weber knew perfectly well, finally, most human actions have consequences *other than those anticipated* by the agents involved, and this even if the actions are performed in a fully deliberate way. The Protestant sectarians of the seventeenth and eighteenth centuries certainly did not 'aim at' the human consequences of modern capitalism as we know them.

In sum, Weber's account of human action provides for a wide spectrum of motives and behaviors. It obviously undermines the claim that to know a society is to understand the 'rules' that govern it; for there are different *kinds* of rules, and different *relationships* between rules and actions. Weber's approach also makes nonsense of the idea that sociologists can only characterize a culture 'in its own terms.' He never abandoned his commitment to the rational individual as the initial hypothesis of the interpretive *method*. Yet his theory of action ultimately extends well beyond this foundation, to a complex model in which behaviors may be not only irrational or

15. Ibid., pp. 12, 15.
16. Ibid., pp. 10–11.

habitual but also largely unconscious—and productive of outcomes that bear little relationship to the motives and beliefs of the agents involved. In short, Weber's methodology did *not* prevent him from dealing with *all* the causes and consequences of human behaviors, any more than it blocked his analysis of social collectivities and structures.

In the Introduction to *Economy and Society,* which was written late in Weber's life, he distinguished the work of the sociologist from that of the historian. He thought it possible to detect "regularities" in the realm of social action, cases in which similar "meanings" lead to similar "progressions" of behavior. Sociology, he argued, is concerned with such "types" of progressions, whereas history engages in the causal analysis of "fateful singular relationships." Here is a more complete formulation of the distinction.

> Sociology develops . . . typological concepts and seeks general rules about events. This in contrast to history, which pursues the causal analysis . . . of individual, culturally significant actions, structures, and personalities. . . . [Sociology] forms its concepts and seeks its rules primarily with a view to whether it can thereby serve the causal attribution of . . . [singular] historical phenomena.

On the one hand, sociology is here plainly described as a generalizing, regularity-seeking discipline, rather than an 'idiographic' one, and its method is said to be essentially typological. A clear line is drawn between the two approaches.[17]

On the other hand, sociology is assigned the task of facilitating the causal analysis of singular historical phenomena. The objects of historical understanding are still contemporary outcomes that strike the investigator as culturally significant in themselves. There is no suggestion that the historian's findings are interesting primarily as elements in the generalizations of the sociologist. While sociology is not subordinated to history, the two disciplines are thoroughly interdefined. The difference between them is more a matter of

17. Ibid., pp. 14, 9.

emphasis than of principle, especially since Weber's account of causal analysis in history *always* encompassed typological tactics and the recourse to 'nomological' knowledge in any case.

This is not to deny that there was a discernible shift in Weber's *practice* during the course of his career, and especially between about 1909 and 1920. Having begun as a legal and economic historian, he gradually became a comparative historical sociologist of religion and of modern capitalism. Broadly theoretical concerns to some extent replaced more specific historical topics in his work. During a 1909 campaign to obtain funds for collaborative sociological investigations, he explicitly challenged the excesses of "historism" *(Historismus)*.[18] He never abandoned his theoretical model of singular causal analysis; but his topics became ever more encompassing in their scope and chronological scale. He also became much more interested in *comparative* tactics, which effectively took the place of *counterfactual* reasoning. The progression was natural and almost inevitable, given his starting point. As the questions he asked about his culture became wider and more radical, his inquiry into its historical antecedents grew virtually universal in scope. At the same time, he began to develop categories and analytical tactics that seemed most likely to prove fruitful in a systematic analysis of the modern world, even when he was unable to carry out his projects in detail.

In that sense, Weber gradually became more a historical sociologist and less a sociologically informed historian. Yet this change of emphasis never forced him to alter the *fundaments* of his methodology. He continued to conceive history as a network of dynamic processes and alternate paths of development. It is surely significant that some of the most committed students of Weber in Germany today are historians, and that it is Weber who has inspired the most significant new direction in contemporary German historiography, a historiography that has pursued the comparative analysis of structural change.[19]

18. See *MWG* II/6, pp. 212–221.

19. I am referring to Hans Ulrich Wehler's *'Gesellschaftsgeschichte'*; but see also Kocka, "Webers Bedeutung," and Mommsen, "Soziologische Geschichte." Roth and Schluchter, the two leading sociologists inspired by Weber, have written on *Weber's Vision of History*.

An Example of Weber's Practice: The Protestant Ethic

I would now like to consider an example of Weber's practice, but I have a tactical problem. I cannot fully discuss any of his substantive works; for that would take me far beyond the realm of methodology. My only option, therefore, is to sketch one of his major texts in terms that, while certainly provisional, may serve to illustrate the practical applications of his methodological canons. With that understanding, I propose to take up the revised version of Weber's *The Protestant Ethic and the Spirit of Capitalism*. In introducing this topic, Weber cited statistics on average incomes, occupations, and educational levels among Protestants and Catholics that had attracted the attention of other commentators as well. His initial question was how to account for the comparative advantage of Protestants around 1900; but he quickly moved on to more complicated issues.[20]

In brief, Weber sought to trace the impact of Protestantism, and especially of the Calvinist sects, upon the *'spirit'* of *'modern capitalism,'* and he only gradually clarified the meaning of these terms—or what it was he proposed to explain. He did *not* regard the religious orientations of his Protestant sectarians as either necessary or sufficient causes of capitalism; but he did believe that these orientations helped to shape the 'spirit' or culture of what he called 'modern' capitalism. Since he ultimately defined both 'modern' capitalism and its 'spirit' in ways that linked them to Protestant forms of this-worldly asceticism, one could perceive his argument as circular.

This perception is quickly corrected, however, if one recalls Weber's view of singular causal analysis. What has to be explained, as he repeatedly observed, is why a certain culturally significant historical outcome became what it has become, *and not something else*. The working out of that question must proceed gradually toward a relevant description of the outcome at issue, even while it projects other possible paths of development by means of counterfactual

20. See *GAR* I, pp. 1–16 ("Vorbemerkung"), and 17–206 ("Die protestantische Ethik und der Geist des Kapitalismus"), revised for republication in 1920, for this and what follows.

and/or comparative reasoning. For Weber, 'modern capitalism' must be distinguished from such earlier phenomena as 'adventure' or 'speculative' capitalism, in that it rests upon distinctive abstractions and forms of rationality. Examples are the separation of household and enterprise, capital accounting and profit calculation, and the systematic organization of formally 'free' labor. The 'spirit' of modern capitalism must not be traced to a presumably natural human yearning for pleasure, luxury, or the satisfaction of desire, for modern capitalists pursue a 'calling' and perform a 'task' in a mood of self-control and self-abnegation. Their 'overall habitus' arises from a systematic rationalization of their 'life conduct' in the light of their 'calling.' And it is their ascetic 'ethic' that really calls for explanation.

Weber explicitly considered the analysis he offered a model of how 'ideas' play a role in history. He noted that the causal relationships he detected were 'adequate,' rather than lawlike. His analytical tactics were most often comparative or counterfactual. He offered probabilistic claims about 'causal chains' and 'tendencies,' rather than deductions from universal generalizations. And the 'elective affinities' he observed were based upon complex mutual *interactions* among attitudes, practices, and institutions. Finally, Weber strenuously rejected the suggestion that he meant to replace a dogmatic historical 'materialism' with an equally dogmatic 'spiritualism.' In support of his position, he not only pointed to the causal interactions that gave rise to 'elective affinities'; he also insisted that the relationship between the religious beliefs of the Protestant ascetics and the secular culture of modern capitalism is very far from linear. The historical record, in other words, is rich in ironic reversals and unintended consequences.

Spelling out his argument, Weber began with the Protestant conception of work as an individual duty or 'calling,' rather than a contribution to an organic order, as in scholastic theology. For Martin Luther and his followers, the idea of a specific vocation came to signify the passive acceptance of the existing sociopolitical system. Among certain Protestant sects, however, a more strenuous and potentially revolutionary vision of action in the world grew out of the Calvinist doctrine of predestination. In logic, the dark creed of gratuitously preordained damnation or 'election' should have led to fatalism. In reality, it typically engendered an unprecedented individual isolation and loneliness in the presence of an inscrutable God. The overwhelming psychological pressures upon the believer could find no relief in confession, absolution, or other forms of institutionalized 'magic'; in that sense, the Calvinist world was thoroughly 'disenchanted.' Individuals had only two ways of dealing with a theology that proved emotionally unbearable. In successfully pursuing a virtuous life, they could seek *symptoms,* if not *causes,* of their place among the divinely elected. Or they could make themselves the instruments of God's glory in this world, most often in religious sects that anticipated the otherworldly fellowship of the saints.

Weber knew perfectly well, of course, that his subject matter extended well beyond the rational implications of theological doctrines; he was interested in attitudes and forms of conduct, not just in formal beliefs. He therefore had to move his analytical focus from the Calvinist theory of predestination to the everyday orientations of such seventeenth- and eighteenth-century Protestant sectarians as the Puritans, orientations he found articulated in the writings of such spiritual counselors as Richard Baxter. Weber recognized that the shift of emphasis to religious practice and feeling was 'psychological' in some sense of that term; but as usual, he expressly excluded the recourse to psychological 'laws' in the style of Karl Lamprecht.

Resting his 'psychological' interpretations upon a commonsense notion of the 'understandable,' Weber could show how work for the glory of God could come to mean work for the common good—and could thus ultimately encourage secular forms of utilitarianism as well. In the same way, he could explain that working in a particular vocation could lead to acceptance of the division of labor and of occupational specialization. Weber's main point about the Protestant sectarians, however, had to do with the human energies released by their religious needs. The tensions inherent in their spiritual situation could not be abreacted through intermittent good works or institutionalized 'magic'; they could only express themselves in the methodical rationalization of their life conduct as a whole. What emerged from the pressures upon them was a combination of self-control and self-denial, a radical indifference to worldly authority, an occasionally unforgiving righteousness, and a determination to transform the world in God's honor.

In short, Weber sought to point up the religious grounding of a compulsion to achieve that had nothing to do with the pursuit of pleasure. A form of this-worldly asceticism and the systematic rationalization of conduct decisively shaped the 'spirit' of 'modern capitalism,' as well as the broader process of rationalization that has made our culture what it is. The darkest passages in Weber's extended essay deal with the erosion of the religious concerns that initially engendered the ethos of this-worldly asceticism. Once in place, Weber argued, the capitalist system no longer needs such religiously grounded energies—or their moral equivalents. For in our own time, individuals can scarcely survive, unless they conform to competitive norms that have come to function independently of their origins. Like marionettes, we are moved by forces beyond our horizons. Our obsession with achievement, our resignation in the face of occupational specialization, and our self-righteous hardness toward those who fail in our eyes: all these have become groundless, 'substantively irrational' in Weber's terms.

From a methodological perspective, *The Protestant Ethic* is probably most interesting as an application of Weber's ideal-typical tactic, which moves the causal analysis forward in three ways. First, Weber posits a model of Calvinist theology that focuses upon the doctrine of predestination and its logical consequences. Since Weber does not share the assumptions of the Calvinist creed, his ideal type of the predestinarian argument is not one of 'right rationality'; but the interpretation it provides is nonetheless a *rational* one. In introducing the heuristic model of Calvinist dogma, Weber does not have to claim that any individual actually believed in it—or acted accordingly. On the contrary, Weber promptly introduces a second ideal type to capture a likely reaction to the dilemmas posed by predestination, a reaction that is 'understandable' in commonsense *psychological* terms. Notice that this second ideal type may be 'adequate at the level of meaning,' even apart from any empirical evidence about the actions and beliefs of real historical agents.

Once again, moreover, Weber does not need to argue that the type is fully applicable to any single individual. All he must show is that it correctly identifies significant aspects of Protestant orientations. Indeed, Weber offers supplementary hypotheses to account for *divergences* of outlook among the members of different sects. To the extent that these ancillary explanations are cogent, they actually strengthen, rather than weaken, his central argument about the 'Protestant ethic' in general. Finally, the ideal-typical method allows Weber to address not only collective 'ideas,' but group attitudes and practices. The ideal Puritan is neither a real nor an average individual, and yet Weber can remain a methodological individualist, even while analyzing a *habitus* that is characteristic of collectivities over extended periods of time. To support his claim about this habitus empirically, Weber does cite statistics; but he also offers textual *interpretations* that really contribute more than any numerical data to the *explanation* of the outcome that interests him.

It is probably safe to say that Weber never wrote anything like 'narrative history,' or any account of specific 'events' in the ordinary sense of the term. He was always primarily a (comparative) historian or historical sociologist of long-term structural change. His *Protestant Ethic* illustrates his persistent emphasis upon historical *processes* and developmental sequences. At every stage of his extended essay, he tries to demonstrate how a set of historical conditions and human experiences gives rise to 'tendencies' that are then channeled into one or more particular paths by ancillary forces or intervening pressures. And while Weber was no 'historical idealist,' at least some of the historical forces he found at work were conceptual or attitudinal in character.

CONCLUSION

—

One way to appreciate Max Weber's extraordinary achievement as a methodologist of the cultural and social sciences is to understand him *historically,* in relation to his own intellectual field. Seen in that way, Weber perfectly typifies the clarifying critic who restates, rationalizes, and thus partly transcends the assumptions of his own culture. This certainly applies to his adaptation of the German historical tradition.

Consider the theme of 'individuality' within that tradition, the enduring sense that the historian is interested in the unique and concretely 'individual', rather than the timelessly 'abstract' and general. In the rhetoric of the Baden neo-Kantians, this emphasis was codified as a contrast between 'idiographic' and 'nomothetic' knowledge. But even to characterize the purely 'individual' is to run the risk of incoherence, since the 'unique' and 'concrete' are inherently indescribable. The only possible 'translation' of the 'individualizing' approach, in fact, is Weber's account of singular causal explanation, in which the 'singular' is not *literally* unique, but conceptualized in a way that makes it subject to causal explanation based partly upon 'rules of experience'. To read Weber is thus actually to *understand* the 'idiographic' strategy, even while recognizing its limitations. Much the same is true of German historical economics. Having stripped away its 'irrationalist' and 'emanationist' accretions, Weber convinces us of its primary thesis: that the 'economic man' of classical theory is an 'ideal type,' not a real human agent. In the light of this insight, Weber could appreciate the neoclassical models of the Austrian school, even while extending German historical economics to a whole new set of topics.

In specifying the case for singular causal explanation, of course, Weber had to deal with the problem of selecting and describing the objects of historical analysis. As we have seen, he simply acknowledged the role of the investigator's personal and cultural interests, without entangling himself in Rickert's pursuit of 'objective' values. For Weber, historians simply identify a striking feature of their own social environment, in order to ask how it came to be what it is, *rather than* something else. The form of this question really contains Weber's whole program of singular causal analysis: against a background of ongoing processes, a cause is something that *intervenes* to modify the path of development—and thus *brings about* an outcome other than what could have been expected in its absence. The idea of processes being channeled into one of several possible directions in turn demands the theory of objective probability and adequate causation, along with counterfactual and/or comparative reasoning. Indeed, it ultimately suggests the comparative analysis of structural change. That is the sense in which Weber's creativity must be conceived as the critical revision of an intellectual heritage, rather than the 'creation' of a 'new idea'—or the linear continuation of an established tradition.

In any case, Weber was *not* simply a follower of Rickert; nor is there any reason to insist that he should have been deeply concerned with Rickert's philosophical obscurities. He simply drew a line between the grounds of the researcher's (possibly subjective) choice of an object of study, typically a significant historical outcome, and the causal explanation of that outcome, which must *aim* at 'objectivity' in principle, though it may fall short of that goal in practice. Although historians certainly construct their questions in the light of their interests, their findings should be valid for other individuals and cultures, partly because the terminology of any culture may be translated into that of another, again *in principle*. Thus altogether, Weber repudiated most of the arguments of the relativists, and his defense of 'objectivity' helped to shape his attitude toward the broader issue of value judgments in science. None of Weber's writings broke as radically with the views prevalent among his colleagues as his polemics on 'value neutrality.' For many members of the Social Policy Association believed in an 'ethical' direction in applied economics. In German academic ideology, moreover, *Wissenschaft* was traditionally supposed to engender *Bildung* and a value-oriented *Weltanschauung*—or in effect to lead beyond knowledge, to wisdom. Weber did not cheerfully abandon that hope; but it seemed to him increasingly unrealistic—and a potential threat to the 'intellectual rectitude' he prized above all.

Just as he both clarified and transcended the idea of an 'individualizing' science, moreover, Weber literally 'made sense' of the doctrine of interpretive 'understanding.' He did this partly by purging the interpretive method of any residual recourse to the empathetic 'reexperiencing' of feeling states, or the subjective *identification* of interpreters with those they seek to understand (by 'putting themselves in their place'). In the face of such temptations, Weber redescribed interpretation as an initially hypothetical construction, in which possibly attributable motives and beliefs are 'tested' against an empirically observable 'progression' of behaviors—or against a pattern of explicit argument. The starting point for this strategy is the heuristic ascription of 'right rationality'; but this is supplemented in a stepwise procedure designed to approximate the complex causal connections between the agent's 'inner' motives and reasons and the 'outward' phenomena they explain. In effect, Weber held that reasons for acting *may be* causes of actions; yet he never claimed that *all* the causes of actions and beliefs are reasons, not to mention good reasons. He was thus necessarily committed to the view that *interpretation is a subset of singular causal explanation.*

The subtitle of this book refers to Weber's 'unification of the cultural and social sciences.' This characterization of his achievement is defensible primarily because he broke through the barrier between interpretation and causal explanation, a barrier that had deep ideological supports in his own culture—and elsewhere as well. But it is of the utmost importance that *he could not have done this under a literally deductive-nomological model* of causal explanation, one in which events that sufficiently (and terminologically) resemble the cause are invariably followed by events that resemble the effect.

Weber knew, after all, that similar reasons may lead to different actions, and that similar actions may follow upon divergent reasons. As we know, he considered this problem serious enough to urge that action explanations, though 'adequate at the level of meaning', may nevertheless require further confirmation in more conventional ways, perhaps even by means of statistics. In any case, he absolutely needed the triadic causal scheme that has been repeatedly sketched above, in which a 'cause' intervenes in a process to 'bring about' an otherwise unexpected 'effect.'

All this helps to account for Weber's distinctive use of the 'ideal type,' which supports his cognitive strategy in at least four respects. First, the ideal type explicitly identifies those aspects of a social or historical pattern that are to be explained. Second, it permits the stepwise approach to the analysis of actions and beliefs, in which ideal types of rational action are supplemented, where necessary, by other 'understandable' reasons, and then by causes other than reasons, until a plurality of hypothetical models jointly suffice to approximate the observed sequence of actions or arguments. Third and analogously, the 'ideal type' allows the cultural or social scientist to 'ascribe' particular aspects of a process or outcome to specific elements within a complex cluster of causes. Fourth and finally, it offers a tentative insight into the relationship between singular causal analysis in human affairs and systematic explanation in the natural sciences. For as Menger observed, explanations in terms of scientific laws are often 'ideal,' in the sense that they abstract from certain aspects of the 'concrete' events to which they apply.

Weber's ideal typical tactics have not always been fully understood, whether in his own time or since. To discuss them at all, however, is to move from a historical assessment of Weber's work in its own intellectual field to a more substantive evaluation of it in contemporary terms. The point of this essay is not to complete such an evaluation, or to formulate a fully coherent philosophy of the cultural and social sciences. But I do mean to claim that Weber's methodology remains remarkably relevant and fruitful even today, more than three-quarters of a century after his death. Following his own recommendation, I have drawn upon particularly cogent contemporary formulations to offer a rational reconstruction of his methodology that provides a starting point for a full interpretation. But to the extent that this approach has been successful, it has also increased my respect for Weber. What it demonstrates, after all, is that he largely anticipated the arguments of MacIntyre and Davidson on causal explanation, and on reasons as causes, just as he anticipated the reflections of Lukes and others on rationality and interpretation. Above all, he *integrated interpretation and explanation,* and he thus successfully challenged a false antithesis that has long been a serious obstacle to thought about the cultural and social world.

Our own intellectual field today is in a state of transition and even of crisis. Changing cultural perspectives and social concerns have inspired new lines of analysis in almost every discipline outside the natural sciences. New questions have been asked about the history of gender roles and of racism, and our studies have pointed up the extraordinary significance of *symbolic* power. As Weber argued, such shifts in perspectives and lines of investigation should be welcomed as sources of vitality, and so should the methodological debates that typically accompany them. Yet to ask an interesting new question is not necessarily to provide a cogent answer. Nor can scholarly claims be defended merely by pointing to the social significance of the issues they address. Indeed, cultural crises may lead to intellectual disorientation as well as to creativity. This was true of the crisis of German academic culture in Weber's own time, and it may be partly true in our own intellectual field.

Perhaps there has been an underlying loss of confidence in the human and social relevance of intellectual work. In Weber's world, there was a widespread conviction that the scholarly community had lost its former authority. Something like a fear of impotence gave rise to the penchant for personal 'prophecy' that Weber so thoroughly distrusted. If I yearn to be a 'true intellectual,' and not a mere 'specialist,' I may be tempted to reach too hastily for morally or ideologically profitable 'truths,' if not for mere novelty. Some of the irrational currents in Weber's environment are not without contemporary parallels; this is true even of the revulsion against 'positivism.' However fruitful Hempel's 'covering law' hypothesis may have proved within the discipline of philosophy, it provoked highly destructive reactions in the cultural and social sciences. Somewhere in our cognitive landscape, the specter of determinism may still be frightening the children within us. Why is it so hard to accept the idea that human action can be *causally* explained, and this most easily when it is most rational and 'free'? And why is it so difficult to see that we understand human 'subjectivity' through its 'objective' manifestations, or that questions grounded in 'subjective' concerns should nonetheless be answered as 'objectively' as possible? Must we quibble forever about the supposed divide between interpretation and explanation, the 'humanities' and the 'social sciences'?

In my own discipline of history, responsible practitioners have continued to think in causal terms. But some of our methodological innovators seem determined to replace causal analysis with surrogates that strike me as hopelessly confused. We are told that the writing of history should be understood as the more or less gratuitous pursuit of literary forms, or that we must return to pure 'narrative,' or engage in interpretive 'description.' Because it is difficult to validate particular interpretations, or because historical knowledge is vaguely perceived as self-referential, we are asked to accept a virulent form of cultural relativism, along with a vision of scholarly debate as an irreconcilable conflict among 'ideologies,' if not among purely personal preferences.

One of the ways in which Weber can help us find a way through our difficulties is to offer an account of causal analysis that will elucidate our best practices much better than Hempel's program. In the process, Weber's methodology should also convince us that both 'descriptions' and 'narratives' cannot be structured—or even *delimited*—without criteria of what is causally relevant to a particular course of events or a specific 'outcome', however complex. Moreover, Weber can show that there must be standards that will allow us *in principle* to defend particular interpretations of actions or texts. Urging us to begin with the hypothetical attribution of rationality, he can demonstrate that we should not look for 'ideology'—or move beyond 'adequacy at the level of meaning'—until we have *shown* that we cannot 'make sense' of what we want to understand *without* recourse to causes other than reasons. (It is hard imagine how we are to discriminate among competing 'deconstructions.')

Finally, Weber may help us to navigate the maelstrom of multiple definitions, thoughtless or deliberate conflations, and irrelevant factual claims that have accumulated around the false antitheses of 'interpretation' and 'explanation,' the 'humanities' (or 'cultural studies') and the 'social sciences,' the 'objective' and the 'subjective.' Of course we should debate our substantive and methodological differences as vigorously as possible. But frankly, I sometimes wonder whether the heat of our purely intra-academic cultural wars may cause us to neglect the norms of reason—and the quest for clarity—that our culture needs more urgently than anything else. Following Weber, I am inclined to conclude with something like a plea for 'intellectual rectitude.'

BIBLIOGRAPHY
INDEX

BIBLIOGRAPHY

—

1. Max Weber's Relevant Writings, with Abbreviations Used

JOURNALS

Archiv = *Archiv für Sozialwissenschaft und Sozialpolitik.*
Jahrbuch = *Jahrbuch für Gesetzgebung, Verwaltung und Volkswirtschaft im Deutschen Reich* [*Schmollers Jahrbuch*].
Logos = *Logos: Internationale Zeitschrift für Philosophie der Kultur.*

COLLECTED WORKS

GAR I = Max Weber, *Gesammelte Aufsätze zur Religionssoziologie*, vol. I (Tübingen: Mohr, 1978) [1st ed., 1920].
GASS = Max Weber, *Gesammelte Aufsätze zur Soziologie und Sozialpolitik* (Tübingen: Mohr, 1988) [1st ed., 1924].
GAW = Max Weber, *Gesammelte Aufsätze zur Wissenschaftslehre*, 4th ed., ed. Johannes Winckelmann (Tübingen: Mohr, 1973) [1st ed. 1922]
MWG I/17 = *Max Weber Gesamtausgabe*, part I, vol. 17: *Wissenschaft als Beruf, 1917/1919; Politik als Beruf, 1919*, ed. Wolfgang J. Mommsen, Wolfgang Schluchter, and Birgitt Morgenbrod (Tübingen: Mohr, 1992).
MWG I/19 = *Max Weber Gesamtausgabe*, part I, vol. 19: *Die Wirtschaftsethik der Weltreligionen: Konfuziamismus und Taoismus: Schriften 1915–1920*, ed. Helwig Schmidt-Glintzer with Petra Kolonko (Tübingen: Mohr, 1989).
MWG II/5 = *Max Weber Gesamtausgabe*, part II, vol. 5: *Briefe 1906–1908*, ed. M. Rainer Lepsius, Wolfgang Mommsen, Birgit Rudhard, and Manfred Schön (Tübingen: Mohr, 1990).

MWG II/6 = *Max Weber Gesamtausgabe*, part II, vol. 6 : *Briefe 1909–1910*, ed. M. Rainer Lepsius, Wolfgang Mommsen, Birgit Rudhard, and Manfred Schön (Tübingen: Mohr, 1994).

W&G = Max Weber, *Wirtschaft und Gesellschaft: Grundriss der verstehenden Soziologie*, 5th ed., ed. Johannes Winckelmann (Tübingen: Mohr, 1976) [first pub. 1921–22].

ESSAYS (IN CHRONOLOGICAL ORDER)

"Roscher" = Max Weber, "Roscher und Knies und die logischen Probleme der historischen Nationalökonomie," part I: "Roschers 'historische Methode,'" in *GAW*, pp. 1–42 [first pub. in *Jahrbuch*, 27 (1903): 1–41].

"Geleitwort" = Werner Sombart, Max Weber, and Edgar Jaffe (as new editors), "Geleitwort," in *Archiv*, 19 (1904): 1–7.

"Objektivität" = Max Weber, "Die 'Objektivität' sozialwissenschaftlicher und sozialpolitischer Erkenntnis," in *GAW*, pp. 146–214 [first pub. in *Archiv*, 19 (1904): 22–87].

"Knies" = Max Weber, "Roscher und Knies und die logischen Probleme der historischen Nationalökonomie," part II: "Knies und das Irrationalitätsproblem," in *GAW*, pp. 42–145 [first pub. in *Jahrbuch*, 29 (1905): 89–150; 30 (1906): 81–120].

"Studien" = Max Weber, "Kritische Studien auf dem Gebiet der kulturwissenschaftlichen Logik," in *GAW*, pp. 215–290 [first pub. in *Archiv*, 22 (1906): 143–207].

"Stammler" = Max Weber, "R. Stammlers 'Überwindung' der materialistischen Geschichtsauffassung," in *GAW*, pp. 291–359 [first pub. in *Archiv*, 24 (1907): 94–151].

"Grenznutzlehre" = Max Weber, "Die Grenznutzlehre und das 'psychophysische Grundgesetz,'" in *GAW*, pp. 384–399 [first pub. in *Archiv*, 27 (1908): 546–558].

"Energetik" = Max Weber, "'Energetische' Kulturtheorien," in *GAW*, pp. 400–426 [first pub. in *Archiv*, 29 (1909): 575–598].

"Aufgaben" = Max Weber, review of Adolf Weber, *Die Aufgaben der Volkswirtschaftslehre als Wissenschaft*, in *Archiv*, 29 (1909): 615–620.

"Diskussion 1909" = Max Weber, Diskussionsbeiträge zu den Verhandlungen "Über die Produktivität der Volkswirtschaft", in *GASS*, pp. 416–423 [first pub. in *Schriften des Vereins für Socialpolitik*, vol. 132: *Verhandlungen der Generalversammlung in Wien . . . Sept. 1909* (Leipzig, 1910)].

"Diskussion 1910" = Max Weber, "Diskussionsreden" zu W. Sombart, 'Technik und Kultur' and zu H. Kantorowicz, 'Rechtswissenschaft und Soziologie,' in *GASS*, pp. 449–456, 476–483 [first pub. in *Verhandlungen des Ersten Deutschen Soziologentages . . . Oktober 1910 in Frankfurt* (Tübingen, 1911)].

"Gutachten" = Max Weber, "Gutachten zur Werturteilsdiskussion im Ausschuss des Vereins für Sozialpolitik," in Eduard Baumgarten, *Max Weber: Werk und Person* (Tübingen: Mohr, 1964), pp. 102–139 [first printed in ms. 1913].

"Kategorien" = Max Weber, "Über einige Kategorien der verstehenden Soziologie," in *GAW*, pp. 427–474, esp. 427–455 [first pub. in *Logos*, vol. 4 (1913), pp. 253–294].

"Einleitung" = Max Weber, "Die Wirtschaftsethik der Weltreligionen. Vergleichende religionssoziologische Versuche. Einleitung," in *MWG*, I/19, pp. 83–127 [first read to friends 1913, first pub. in *Archiv*, 41 (1915): 1–87].

"Wertfreiheit" = Max Weber, "Der Sinn der 'Wertfreiheit' der soziologischen und ökonomischen Wissenschaften," in *GAW*, pp. 489–540 [first pub. in *Logos*, vol. 7 (1917), pp. 40–88].

"Wissenschaft" = Max Weber, "Wissenschaft als Beruf," in *MWG* I/17, pp. 71–111 [first pub. as printed lecture in series 'Geistige Arbeit als Beruf' (Munich, 1919)].

"Grundbegriffe" = Max Weber, "Soziologische Grundbegriffe," in *W&G*, pp. 1–30, esp. pp. 1–20.

"Nachtrag" = "Nachtrag zu dem Aufsatz über R. Stammlers 'Überwindung' der materialistischen Geschichtsauffassung," in *GAW*, pp. 360–380 [first pub. in 1922 *GAW*].

ENGLISH TRANSLATIONS (IN CHRONOLOGICAL ORDER)

Weber, Max, *From Max Weber: Essays in Sociology*, trans. and ed. H. H. Gerth and C. Wright Mills (New York: Oxford University Press, 1946), contains: "Science as a Vocation" [= "Wissenschaft"], pp. 129–156.

Weber, Max, *The Methodology of the Social Sciences*, trans. and ed. Edward A. Shils and Henry A. Finch (New York: Free Press, 1949) contains: "The Meaning of 'Ethical Neutrality' in Sociology and Economics" [= "Wertfreiheit"], pp. 1–47;

"'Objectivity' in Social Science and Social Policy" [= "Objektivität"], pp. 50–112;

"Critical Studies in the Logic of the Cultural Sciences" [= "Studien"], pp. 113–188.

Weber, Max, *Economy and Society*, ed. Guenther Roth and Claus Wittich, vol. I (Berkeley: University of California Press, 1978), contains: "Basic Sociological Terms" [= "Grundbegriffe"], pp. 3–56; see esp. pp. 3–38.

I know of no other relevant English translations that can be recommended with confidence.

2. Other Primary Sources

Dilthey, Wilhelm, *Einleitung in die Geisteswissenschaften* [*Gesammelte Schriften*, vol. I] (Stuttgart: Teubner, 1990), pp. 3–120.

Dilthey, Wilhelm, "Ideen zu einer vergleichenden und zergliedernden Psychologie," in *Gesammelte Schriften*, vol. V, pp. 139–240.

Dilthey, Wilhelm, *Der Aufbau der geschichtlichen Welt in den Geisteswissenschaften* [*Gesammelte Schriften*, vol. VII], pp. 79–220.

Droysen, Johann Gustav, *Grundriss der Historik*, 3rd ed. [1882], in Droysen, *Historik*, ed. Peter Leyh (Stuttgart: Frommann-Holzboog, 1977), pp. 415–488.

Jellinek, Georg, *Das Recht des modernen Staates*, vol. I : *Allgemeine Staatslehre* (Berlin, 1900), esp. pp. 3–39.

Knies, Karl, *Die politische Oekonomie vom Standpunkte der geschichtlichen Methode* (Braunschweig, 1853), esp. pp. 1–35, 70–123, 321–355.

Kries, Johannes von, "Ueber den Begriff der objektiven Möglichkeit," *Vierteljahrsschrift für wissenschaftliche Philosophie*, 12 (1888): 180–240, 289–323, 394–428, esp. 180–220.

Lamprecht, Karl, *Moderne Geschichtswissenschaft: Fünf Vorträge* (Freiburg im Breisgau, 1905), esp. pp. 1–76.

Lange, Friedrich Albert, *Geschichte des Materialismus und Kritik seiner Bedeutung in der Gegenwart* (Iserlohn, 1866), esp. pp. iii–xiv, 233–557.

Menger, Carl, *Untersuchungen über die Methode der Socialwissenschaften und der Politischen Oekonomie insbesondere* (Leipzig, 1883), esp. pp. 3–59.

Meyer, Eduard, *Zur Theorie und Methodik der Geschichte* (Halle, 1902).

Radbruch, Gustav, *Die Lehre von der adäquaten Verursachung* [Abhandlungen des kriminalistischen Seminars an der Universität Berlin] (Berlin, 1902), pp. 325–408, esp. pp. 333–337.

Ranke, Leopold von, *Die grossen Mächte*, ed. Friedrich Meinecke (Leipzig, 1916), pp. 13–61.

Ranke, Leopold von, *Das politische Gespräch und andere Schriften zur Wissenschaftslehre* (Halle, Saale, 1925), pp. 10–36.

Rickert, Heinrich, *Die Grenzen der naturwissenschaftlichen Begriffsbildung* (Tübingen, 1902).

Ritschl, Otto, *Die Causalbetrachtung in den Geisteswissenschaften* (Bonn, 1901), esp. pp. 43–89.

Simmel, Georg, "Der Begriff und die Tragödie der Kultur," in his *Philosophische Kultur: Gesammelte Essais* (Leipzig, 1911), pp. 245–277.

Simmel, Georg, *Die Probleme der Geschichtsphilosophie: Eine erkenntnistheoretische Studie* (Leipzig, 1892).

Troeltsch, Ernst, *Naturrecht und Humanität in der Weltpolitik: Vortrag bei der zweiten Jahresfeier der Deutschen Hochschule für Politik* (Berlin, 1923).

Windelband, Wilhelm, "Geschichte und Naturwissenschaft," in *Präludien*, 3rd ed. (Tübingen, 1907), pp. 355–379.

Windelband, Wilhelm, *Die Philosophie im deutschen Geistesleben des 19. Jahrhunderts* (Tübingen, 1927).

3. Contemporary Formulations

Davidson, Donald, "Actions, Reasons, and Causes," in Davidson, *Essays on Actions and Events* (Oxford: Clarendon Press, 1980), pp. 3–19.

Grünbaum, Adolf, *Philosophical Problems of Space and Time* (New York: Knopf, 1963), pp. 281–313.

Hart, H. L. A., and A. M. Honore, *Causation in the Law* (Oxford: Clarendon Press, 1959), esp. pp. 8–57, 412–418.

Hempel, Carl G., "Aspects of Scientific Explanation," in Hempel, *Aspects of Scientific Explanation and Other Essays in the Philosophy of Science* (New York: Free Press, 1965), esp. pp. 331–370, 415–425.

Hempel, Carl G., "Explanation in Science and History," in R. Colodny, ed., *Frontiers of Science and Philosophy* (Pittsburgh, 1962), pp. 7–34.

Hempel, Carl G., "The Function of General Laws in History" [1942], in Hempel, *Aspects of Scientific Explanation*, pp. 231–243.

Hempel, Carl G., "Reasons and Covering Laws in Historical Explanation," in Patrick Gardiner, ed., *The Philosophy of History* (New York: Oxford University Press, 1974), pp. 90–105.

Hollis, Martin, and Steven Lukes, eds., *Rationality and Relativism* (Cambridge, Mass.: MIT Press, 1982).

Lukes, Steven, "Relativism in Its Place," in Hollis and Lukes, eds., *Rationality and Relativism*, pp. 261–305.

MacIntyre, Alasdair, "The Antecedents of Action," in MacIntyre, *Against the Self-Images of the Age: Essays on Ideology and Philosophy* (Notre Dame, Ind.: University of Notre Dame, 1978), pp. 191–210.

MacIntyre, Alasdair, "The Idea of a Social Science," in Bryan R. Wilson, ed., *Rationality*, Key Concepts in the Social Sciences (New York: Harper and Row, 1970), pp. 112–130.

Mackie, J. L., *The Cement of the Universe: A Study of Causation* (Oxford: Clarendon Press, 1974).

Ringer, Fritz, "Causal Analysis in Historical Reasoning," *History and Theory*, 28 (1989): 154–172.

Ringer, Fritz, *Fields of Knowledge: French Academic Culture in Comparative Perspective, 1890–1929* (Cambridge: Cambridge University Press, 1992), pp. 1–25.

Salmon, Wesley C., *Four Decades of Scientific Explanation* (Minneapolis: University of Minnesota Press, 1989).

Salmon, Wesley C., *Scientific Explanation and the Causal Structure of the World* (Princeton: Princeton University Press, 1984).

Salmon, Wesley C., "Why Ask, 'Why?'? : An Inquiry Concerning Scientific Explanation," in Salmon, ed., *Hans Reichenbach: Logical Empiricist* (Boston: Reidel, 1979), pp. 403–425.

Wilson, Bryan R., ed., *Rationality*, Key Concepts in the Social Sciences (New York: Harper and Row, 1970).

Winch, Peter, *The Idea of a Social Science and Its Relation to Philosophy* (New York: Humanities Press, 1958).

4. Selected Secondary Works on Weber's Methodology and Its Context

Bruun, H. H., *Science, Values, and Politics in Max Weber's Methodology* (Copenhagen: Munksgaard, 1972).

Burger, Thomas, "Deutsche Geschichtstheorie und Webersche Soziologie," in Gerhard Wagner and Heinz Zipprian, eds., *Max Webers Wissenschaftslehre: Interpretation und Kritik* (Frankfurt: Suhrkamp, 1994), pp. 29–97.

Burger, Thomas, *Max Weber's Theory of Concept Formation: History, Laws, and Ideal Types* (Durham, N.C.: Duke University Press, 1987).

Chickering, Roger, *Karl Lamprecht: A German Academic Life (1856–1915)* (Atlantic Highlands, N.J.: Humanities Press, 1993).

Ermarth, Michael, *Wilhelm Dilthey: The Critique of Historical Reason* (Chicago: University of Chicago Press, 1975), esp. pp. 3–178.

Forman, Paul, "Weimar Culture, Causality, and Quantum Theory, 1918–1927: Adaptation by German Physicists and Mathematicians to a Hostile Intellectual Environment", reprinted from *Historical Studies in the Physical Sciences*, vol. 3 (1971), by University of Pennsylvania Press.

Hennis, Wilhelm, "Eine Wissenschaft vom Menschen: Max Weber und die deutsche Nationalökonomie der Historischen Schule," in Hennis, *Max Webers Fragestellung: Studien zur Biographie des Werks* (Tübingen: Mohr, 1987), pp. 117–166.

Hennis, Wilhelm, "'Die volle Nüchternheit des Urteils': Max Weber zwischen Carl Menger und Gustav von Schmoller: Zum hochschulpolitischen Hintergrund des Wertfreiheitspostulats," in Wagner and Zipprian, *Max Webers Wissenschaftslehre*, pp. 105–143.

Henrich, Dieter, *Die Einheit der Wissenschaftslehre Max Webers* (Tübingen, 1952).

Iggers, Georg, *The German Conception of History: The National Tradition of Historical Thought from Herder to the Present* (Middletown, Conn.: Wesleyan University Press, 1968).

Käsler, Dirk, *Einführung in das Studium Max Webers* (Munich: Beck, 1979).

Kalberg, Stephen, *Max Weber's Comparative-Historical Sociology* (Chicago: University of Chicago Press, 1994).

Kocka, Jürgen, "Max Webers Bedeutung für die Geschichtswissenschaft," in Kocka, ed., *Max Weber, der Historiker* (Göttingen: Vandenhoeck, 1986), pp. 13–27.

Köhnke, Klaus Christian, *Entstehung und Aufstieg des Neukantianismus: Die deutsche Universitätsphilosophie zwischen Idealismus und Positivismus* (Frankfurt: Suhrkamp, 1986), esp. pp. 233–432.

Löwith, Karl, *Max Weber and Karl Marx,* trans. H. Fantel, ed. T. Bottomore, and W. Outhwaite (London: Allen & Unwin, 1982).

Mommsen, Wolfgang J., "Ideal Type and Pure Type: Two Variants of Max Weber's Ideal-Typical Method," in Mommsen, *The Political and Social Theory of Max Weber: Collected Essays* (Chicago: University of Chicago Press, 1989), pp. 121–132.

Mommsen, Wolfgang J., "Soziologische Geschichte und historische Soziologie," in Mommsen, *Max Weber: Gesellschaft, Politik, und Geschichte,* 2nd ed. (Frankfurt: Suhrkamp, 1982), pp. 182–207.

Oakes, Guy, *Weber and Rickert: Concept Formation in the Cultural Sciences* (Cambridge, Mass.: MIT Press, 1988).

Ringer, Fritz, *The Decline of the German Mandarins: The German Academic Community, 1890–1933* (Hanover, N.H.: Wesleyan University Press and University Press of New England, 1990), pp. 81–180, 253–366.

Ringer, Fritz, *Fields of Knowledge: French Academic Culture in Historical Perspective, 1890–1920* (Cambridge: Cambridge University Press, 1992), pp. 95–108, 196–207.

Ringer, Fritz, *Die Gelehrten: Der Niedergang der deutschen Mandarine, 1890–1933* (Stuttgart: Klett, 1983).

Roth, Guenther, and Wolfgang Schluchter, *Max Weber's Vision of History: Ethics and Methods* (Berkeley: University of California Press, 1979).

Runciman, W. G., *A Critique of Max Weber's Philosophy of Social Science* (Cambridge: Cambridge University Press, 1972).

Schelting, Alexander von, *Max Webers Wissenschaftslehre: Das logische Problem der historischen Kulturerkenntnis. Die Grenzen der Soziologie des Wissens* (Tübingen, 1934).

Smith, Woodruff D., *Politics and the Science of Culture in Germany, 1840–1920* (New York: Oxford University Press, 1991).

Tenbruck, Friedrich H., "Die Genesis der Methodologie Max Webers," *Kölner Zeitschrift für Soziologie und Sozialpsychologie,* 2 (1959): 573–630.

Tenbruck, Friedrich H., "Max Weber und Eduard Meyer," in Wolfgang Mommsen and Wolfgang Schwentker, eds., *Max Weber und seine Zeitgenossen* (Göttingen: Vandenhoeck, 1988), pp. 337–379.

Tenbruck, Friedrich H., "Die Wissenschaftslehre Max Webers: Voraussetzungen zu ihrem Verständnis," in Wagner and Zipprian, *Max Webers Wissenschaftslehre,* pp. 367–389.

Turner, Bryan S., *For Weber: Essays on the Sociology of Fate* (Boston: Routledge, 1981).

Turner, Stephen P., and Regis A. Factor, *Max Weber: The Lawyer as Social Thinker* (New York: Routledge, 1994), esp. pp. 119–165.

Turner, Stephen P., and Regis A. Factor, "Objective Possibility and Adequate Causation in Weber's Methodological Writings," *Sociological Review,* 29 (1981): 5–28.

Vierhaus, Rudolf, "Bildung," in Otto Brunner, Wener Conze, and Reinhard Kosellek, eds., *Geschichtliche Grundbegriffe*, vol. 1 (Stuttgart: Klett, 1972), pp. 508–551.

Wagner, Gerhard, and Heinz Zipprian, eds., *Max Webers Wissenschaftslehre: Interpretation und Kritik* (Frankfurt: Suhrkamp, 1994).

Wagner, Gerhard, and Heinz Zipprian, "Methodologie und Ontologie: Zum Problem kausaler Erklärung bei Max Weber," *Zeitschrift für Soziologie*, 14 (1985): 115–130.

Weiss, Johannes, "Kausale Durchsichtigkeit," in Wagner and Zipprian, *Max Webers Wissenschaftslehre*, pp. 507–526.

INDEX

—

Absolutism of theory, 12–13
Actions, 100–101, 106–108, 110, 142–143, 157–160, 171
Adequate causation, 3–4, 50, 63–74, 94, 96, 99, 169
Affectual action, 106
Alternate historical paths, 73, 75, 78, 83, 91
Analogies, diachronic/synchronic, 14
Anarchism, 132–133
Anthropomorphism, 77
Archiv für Sozialwissenschaft und Sozialpolitik, 127–128

Baden school, 21, 32, 43, 168
Barnes, Barry, 147
Bastian, Adolf, 20
Baudelaire, Charles, 139
Baxter, Richard, 165
Beliefs, 143, 148–149, 157–158, 161, 170–171
Below, Georg von, 24, 47
Bildung, 7–9, 11, 19, 43, 120, 124, 134, 170
Bismarck, Otto von, 43–44, 67
Bloor, David, 147
Bourdieu, Pierre, 5, 154–155
Brentano, Lujo, 54, 96–97
Bruun, H. H., 51, 141
Buckle, H. T., 12
Buddhism, 152
Burckhardt, Jakob, 23
Burger, Thomas, 51, 61

Calvinism, 163–166
Capitalism, 151, 156, 160, 163–164, 166
Causal analysis. *See* Singular causal analysis
Causal interactions, 88–90
Causalism, 3–4, 57, 62–63, 75, 93, 99
Causal laws, 40, 64, 74–75
Causal processes, 87–90
Causes: accidental, 65, 69; long-term/short-term, 79
Charity, principle of, 147–148
Chickering, Roger, 23
Christianity, 13, 124, 139, 152–153
Classical economic theory, 12, 56, 60, 114, 168–169
Comparative analysis, 91, 110, 162
Comte, Auguste, 20–21, 53
Confucianism, 152
Constant conjunction, 78, 82
Counterfactual analysis, 69–71, 73, 75–76, 78–79, 84, 91, 110, 114, 162
Courses of events, 76–79, 83, 86
Covering laws, 85, 117, 143–144, 172
Creative synthesis, 55
Culture, 41–43, 48–49

Darwin, Charles, 53
Davidson, Donald, 85, 142–144, 147, 172
Description, problem of, 35
Descriptions of singular objects, 73
Descriptive psychology, 27, 29, 34
Determinism, 12, 21, 25–26, 40, 47, 57–59, 69, 75, 90–91, 150, 173
Deuten. See Interpretation

Deviations, from right rationality, 107–109, 114, 116
Dilthey, Wilhelm, 11, 26–29, 34, 37–38, 43
Divergences, in courses of events, 76–79, 83, 86, 114
Droysen, Johann Gustav, 11–12, 61
Durkheim, Emile, 57, 109, 133, 157

Economics, 12–17, 54–56, 97, 113–114, 151–152, 168–169
Elective affinities, 154–155
Emanationism, 56, 159
Emissary prophecy, 154
Empathetic reproduction, 120, 170
Empathetic understanding, 92, 96
Empathy: principle of, 9–10, 34; role of, 105–106
Empirical generalizations, 75
Empirical laws, 17
Empiricism, 19–21, 31–33, 42, 45, 59, 138, 167
Energetic theory, 53–54
Enlightenment, 24, 44
Ereigniswissenschaften, 32
Essentialism, 52, 56, 60, 112
Ethical neutrality, 51
Event-statement, 72, 79–81
Evidenz, 105–106
Explanandum, 72, 79–81
Explanans, 80–81
Explanation, 92–93, 118, 142, 148, 167, 170, 172, 174
Explanatory approach, 1–3, 5
Expression, 27, 93

Factor, Regis, 50
Folk psychology, 96, 109
Forman, Paul, 25–26
Frederick the Great, 67, 80
Free will, 57–59
Freie Studentenschaft, 131

Geistewissenschaften, 18, 27, 37–39
Generalizations, 75, 81, 83, 111
German historical tradition, 8–17, 46, 52, 56–57, 59–62, 152, 168–169
Gesetzewissenschaften, 31–32, 34, 45, 72, 122
Goethe, Johann Wolfgang von, 43–44, 98, 124
Grandy, Richard, 148

Habitus, 154–155, 167
Hart, H. L. A., 82–83
Hegel, Georg Wilhelm Friedrich, 11, 19, 28, 37, 56
Hempel, Carl G., 2–3, 80–81, 85–86, 89, 117, 172–173
Hennis, Wilhelm, 60–61, 141
Henrich, Dieter, 51, 116–117
Herder, Johann Gottfried von, 23
Hierarchy of sciences, 53
Historical economics, 12–13, 56, 168–169
Historical individuals, 39–41, 47
Historical materialism, 150–151
Historical paths, alternate, 73, 75, 78, 83, 91
Historicism, problem of, 9, 162
History, 38–40, 161–162
Holism, 52, 56–57, 60
Honore, A. M., 82–83
Humanistic disciplines, revival of, 18, 26–35
Humanity, principle of, 148
Humboldt, Wilhelm von, 9
Hume, David, 2, 21, 30, 65, 80–82, 89

Ideal interests, 153
Idealism, 7–8, 11, 19–23, 43–44, 52, 61–62, 167
Ideal types, 5–6, 51, 102, 108, 110–121, 157–158, 166, 168, 171
Idiographic knowledge, 32, 34, 37, 71–72, 168
Immediate experience, 27
Immediate understanding, 103–104
Indeterminism, 89–90
Individuality, principle of, 9–11, 32, 43–44, 56, 60, 168
Intellectual field, 5–6, 8, 18, 45, 168, 171–172
Interactions, causal, 88–90
Interpretation, 37, 43, 50, 57, 92–93, 102, 104–110, 117–120, 125–126, 142, 146–148, 157, 167, 170, 172, 174
Interpretive approach, 1–3, 5
Interpretive sociology, 92, 100–110, 115
Interpretive understanding, 1, 27–29, 92–93, 102, 170
INUS condition, 81–82, 84
Irrationalism, 52, 57, 59–60
Irrationality, 106
Islam, 152

Jaffe, Edgar, 127
Jellinek, Georg, 110–111

Kalberg, Stephen, 155
Kant, Immanuel, 9, 19, 21, 23, 32, 40, 43, 58, 134, 141, 168
Kistiakowski, Theodor, 77
Knies, Karl, 12–15, 25, 56–57, 60, 68, 76, 93–95
Köhnke, Klaus Christian, 19
Kries, Johannes von, 50, 63–67, 69, 76–79, 84

Lamprecht, Karl, 20, 22–24, 53, 55–56, 61–62, 165
Lange, Friedrich Albert, 19, 134
Laws: empirical, 17; in history, 30–31; universal, 37, 46; causal, 40, 64, 74–75; covering, 85, 117, 143–144, 172; as rules, 99–100
LeBon, Gustave, 158
Leipzig Circle, 20, 53, 55
Löwith, Karl, 150–151
Lukes, Steven, 147–148, 172
Luther, Martin, 44, 164

MacIntyre, Alasdair, 83–84, 142–143, 145–146, 172
Mackie, J. L., 81–82, 84
Manchesterites, 129, 132
Mannheim, Karl, 155
Marginal utility, theory of, 16, 54, 97, 113
Marx, Karl, 124, 150–151
Marxism, 20, 113, 132, 146, 150–151
Material interests, 153
Materialism, 150–151
Maxims, 99–100
Meinecke, Friedrich, 24, 57
Menger, Carl, 16–17, 26, 31, 51, 55, 97, 102, 110–111, 171
Methodological individualism, 155–162
Meyer, Eduard, 24–25, 45, 47, 57–58, 66–70, 73, 76, 124–125
Mill, John Stuart, 9, 58, 77, 82–83, 134
Mohl, Robert von, 61–62
Mommsen, Wolfgang, 118–120
Motives, 93–95, 98, 109, 114, 116–117, 142, 161, 170

Naturalism, 52–56, 60–61, 112
Natural rights, 60

Nietzsche, Friedrich, 138–139, 153
Nomological knowledge, 14, 29, 40, 64, 72–73, 76–77, 79, 85, 118, 162
Nomothetic knowledge, 32–34, 37, 168
Norms, 99, 133

Oakes, Guy, 51
Objectification, 28
Objective probability, 3, 50, 63–73, 77, 91, 169
Objectivity, 42, 49–51, 122–123, 125–127, 133, 169, 173–174
Organicism, 52, 56, 60, 159
Ostwald, Wilhelm, 20–21, 53–56

Panofsky, Erwin, 155
Philosophy of life, 27
Plato, 138
Positivism, 6, 12, 17–26, 33, 43, 52, 56, 60–62, 75, 118, 172
Predestination, 165–166
Probabilistic knowledge, 64–65, 69
Progress, 31, 53, 136–137
Progressions of behaviors, 94, 101, 108–109, 114–116, 161, 170
Protestant ethic, 160, 163–167
Psychologism, 20–21, 54–55
Psychology, 20, 54, 109; descriptive, 27, 29, 34; folk, 96, 109
Pure types, 102, 118, 157
Puritans, 165, 167
Purposely rational action, 106–108

Radbruch, Gustav, 66
Ranke, Leopold von, 10–12, 43
Rational action, 106
Rational interpretation, 146–147
Rationality, 4, 6, 57, 59, 96–98, 106–109, 114–116, 137, 141, 147–148. See also Right rationality
Ratzel, Friedrich, 20
Reality, 36–39, 45–46, 63, 71, 112
Real types, 17
Reasons, 148–149
Regression analysis, 84
Regularities, 144–146, 161
Relatively historical concepts, 39
Religion, 152–155
Renaissance, 138
Rickert, Heinrich von, 21, 25, 29, 32, 35–52, 75, 122–124, 127, 131, 138, 141, 169

Riehl, Wilhelm Heinrich, 23
Right rationality, 97–98, 106–109,
    114–116, 118, 120, 137, 147–148,
    166, 170
Romanticism, 9, 24, 157
Roscher, Wilhelm, 12, 56–57, 61
Rules, 99–100, 144–146
Runciman, W. G., 51, 117–118

Salmon, Wesley, 86–90, 156
Savigny, Friedrich von, 12
Schelting, Alexander von, 72
Schmoller, Gustav, 12, 15–16, 47, 54,
    57–58, 128, 132, 134, 141
Science, 53, 75, 87, 117
Sermon on the Mount, 124, 139
Simmel, Georg, 29–31, 34, 38, 40,
    43, 45–46, 50–51, 71, 93–95, 136,
    156
Singular causal analysis, 3–4, 47, 63, 67,
    69–80, 88–92, 99, 114–116,
    118–120, 125, 155–156, 161,
    168–171, 173
Smith, Woodruff, 20
Social action, 101, 157–161
Social Darwinism, 53
Socialism, 136
Socialists of the Lectern, 129
Social Policy Association, 15, 51, 122,
    127, 129–131, 135, 151, 170
Social relationships, 159
Sociology, 107, 157; interpretive, 92,
    100–110, 115; defined, 100–101;
    and history, 161–162
Sombart, Werner, 127, 129
Spirit of the people, 13, 56
Stammler, Rudolf, 57–58, 75, 99–100,
    144, 146, 151
Statistical relevance, 86–87
Subjective rationality, 148
Subjectivity, 42, 49–51, 95, 124–127,
    173–174

Tarde, Gabriel, 158
Teleology, 93–94
Tenbruck, Friedrich, 51, 60–62
Tolstoy, Leo, 138, 140
Traditional action, 106
Transcendental subjectivism, 42
Treitschke, Heinrich von, 57, 61, 132
Troeltsch, Ernst, 9–10
Turner, Stephen, 50

Understanding, 27–30, 43, 50, 92–93,
    96, 102–105, 116–117, 125, 157.
    See also Interpretive understanding
Universal laws, 37, 46

Value analysis, 124–125, 138
Value neutrality, 122, 131–141, 170
Value rational action, 106
Values/value judgments, 8–9, 40–43,
    48, 55, 123–131, 133–134,
    136–138, 141
Verein für Sozialpolitik. *See* Social Policy
    Association
Verstehen. *See* Interpretive understanding
Vienna Circle, 20
Virchow, Rudolf, 20
Vital experience, 136

Weber, Adolf, 129
Weber-Fechner law, 54
Weiss, Johannes, 72
Weltanschauung, 19, 21, 23, 43, 53, 55,
    132, 170
Winch, Peter, 144–146
Windelband, Wilhelm, 21, 29, 31–35,
    37, 43, 45
Wirklichkeitswissenschaften, 31, 34, 38,
    45–46, 72, 122
Wissenschaften, 8, 19, 21, 26, 43, 45,
    131, 137–138, 141, 170
Wittgenstein, Ludwig, 144
Wundt, Wilhelm, 20–23, 53, 55–56